For His Glory

For His Glory

Devotional Notes of Love and Truth

A genuine heart's cry and journey with the Lord

By Darlene Harkins

XULON ELITE

Xulon Press Elite
2301 Lucien Way #415
Maitland, FL 32751
407.339.4217
www.xulonpress.com

© 2022 by Darlene Harkins

All rights reserved solely by the author. The author guarantees all contents are original and do not infringe upon the legal rights of any other person or work. No part of this book may be reproduced in any form without the permission of the author. The views expressed in this book are not necessarily those of the publisher.

Due to the changing nature of the Internet, if there are any web addresses, links, or URLs included in this manuscript, these may have been altered and may no longer be accessible. The views and opinions shared in this book belong solely to the author and do not necessarily reflect those of the publisher. The publisher, therefore, disclaims responsibility for the views or opinions expressed within the work.

Unless otherwise indicated, Scripture quotations taken from the King James Version (KJV)–*public domain.*

Scripture quotations taken from the New King James Version (NKJV). Copyright © 1982 by Thomas Nelson, Inc. Used by permission. All rights reserved.

Scripture quotations taken from the Holy Bible, New International Version (NIV). Copyright © 1973, 1978, 1984, 2011 by Biblica, Inc.™. Used by permission. All rights reserved.

Scripture quotations taken from the English Standard Version (ESV). Copyright © 2001 by Crossway, a publishing ministry of Good News Publishers. Used by permission. All rights reserved.

Paperback ISBN-13: 978-1-66285-993-9
Hardback ISBN-13: 978-1-6628-6195-6
Ebook ISBN-13: 978-1-66285-994-6

Dedicated to

Our heavenly Father God, for His kingdom to be used for His glory.

My husband Brian, a dedicated and faithful man of God. He always encouraged, supported, and prayed over each devotional and prayerfully supported the idea of capturing them all in a book for the body of Christ, all for God's glory.

To family and friends in the body of Christ who encouraged and shared these little notes over the years within their communities, families, and workplaces, even reaching across the globe. You know who you are!

Acknowledgment

Thank you to Mari Enriquez Photography
for assistance with the cover photo.

Preface

This book contains a collection of personal devotionals and is the result of a genuine and true heart's cry to live a life for God's glory.

It all started simply with a desire to dive into the Word in a different way during my personal studies. As the Lord would lead every week, a specific scripture or concept would be the focus of my personal study. In the midst of a busy life and fast-paced world—marriage, family, home, ministry work, friends, and a career as a business executive and leader—I needed the Lord's help in balancing my time with Him. Honestly, I just wanted to slow down, maximize my time, and *commune* with the Lord and take my time to hear from Him. In addition to my daily morning time with Him, I would take the scripture or concept and write it on a Post-it. At the time, I was driving an hour to and from my corporate job and would stick the note on the dashboard of my car. It allowed me additional time to meditate, pray, talk to the Lord, and listen to what He wanted to say to me about it. I soon found that the scripture of focus was relevant for sharing with others as the Lord would lead in many of my daily interactions. I started taking pictures of my personal Post-it notes for easy access and reference. My husband started to notice the notes and commented on how much he liked them, which resulted in the request to send them each to him. It wasn't long after that he encouraged me to start sharing these weekly studies with our church women's group, which I still teach today. This led to sharing them with believers in the workplace, and only the Lord knows how far they have reached. My prayer each week became "Where do we go in Your Word this week, and what do You want to say to me and to Your people, Lord?"

The recommended approach for this personal study and journey with the Lord is simple: By design, there is not a specific date assigned to each devotional. The intent is to take the time you need personally for each devotional study and let the Lord speak to you. The Lord may have you spend a day, days, a week, or weeks on one. Let Him lead you and *commune* with Him.

- Make time and space to commune with our Lord with an open and pure heart.
- Explore the Word. Let the Lord guide you to understand the context. Understanding context means to take the time to understand the setting, audience, timeline, circumstances, or idea of what is written. Take the time to read scripture before and after the provided scripture, note the book you are in and where it is located in the Word. Ensure you understand

relevance, and concept of the scripture. Cross reference scripture with scripture to gain understanding.
- For quick access, consider copying the highlighted notes on each devotional to your own Post-it note or journal. You can also take a picture for quick reference.
- Meditate and pray over it.
- Talk to God about it. Sit at His table. <u>Ask Him three questions:</u>
    1. "What do you want to say to me, Lord?"
    2. "How is this relevant in my own life, Lord?"
    3. "What do You want me to do with this learning, Lord?"
- Consider journaling your thoughts, notes, and responses to each question.
- Once these three questions are answered, you are ready to move on to the next devotional.

God's Word is absolute, everlasting, and powerful. Jesus Christ is the same yesterday, today, and forever **(Heb. 13:8 New King James Version).** However, the journey to walk with Him is unique for each of us as designed by Him according to His plan. I'm praying that the Lord uses these devotionals to give you focus in your time with Him and that as your relationship with Him deepens, much fruit is produced through you for His glory and kingdom!

Join me with an honest desire and a genuine heart's cry unto the Lord in:

- *Believing* who God is and that He has no boundaries in His might or gentleness.
- *Believing* in His Son Jesus and the good work He did on the cross for our sanctification, salvation, and eternal life. Believing is not just saying it is true; it is boldly *walking* and *living* in the truth by His great and promised Spirit.
- *Humbly waiting* on God, *receiving* all He has to offer, and *going forward* as He leads.
- *Reflecting* on these studies and standing where He has us.

Help me be a missionary right here at home and wherever You direct my hands and feet, Lord. Make me Your vessel, Lord. Help me have a pure and clean heart that is willing to be an offering poured out to you (*See* **2 Tim. 4:6 NKJV**). Help me be a sweet-smelling aroma of Your presence (*See* **2 Cor. 2:1–15**). Make me a light in the darkness (*See* **Matt, 5:14–16**).

Take these moments of personal study and prayer and use them for Your glory, Lord!

"Do your *best* to present yourself to God as one approved, a worker who has no need to be ashamed, rightly handling the word of truth" **(2 Tim. 2:15 emphasis added English Standard Version).**

"So he answered and said to me: 'This is the word of the Lord to Zerubbabel, saying: 'Not by might nor by power, but by My Spirit,' says the Lord of hosts" **(Zech. 4:6 NKJV).**

By God's grace, a second volume of devotionals will be published. Be on the watch for the next publiation!

Contents

Living for His Glory.. xvii

Who Are We in God? 1
I Have Access to God's Wisdom 2
The Holy Spirit Lives in Me 3
I Am Helped by God.. 4
I Am Reconciled to God.. 5
I Am Tenderly Loved by God.. 6
We Are Children of God 7
We Are the Sweet Fragrance of Christ to God........................... 8
We Are God's Living Stones.. 9
We Are Part of God's Holy Nation 10
We Are Salt of the Earth 11
We Are Light in This World 12
My Needs Are Met by God 13
Great and Precious Promises of God 14

Who Is Christ in Us?... 15
The Way, the Truth, and the Life..................................... 16
We Are Branches on Christ's Vine 17
The Indwelling and Outpouring of the Holy Spirit..................... 18
Jesus Is Our Friend.. 20
A Spirit of Power, Love, and a Sound Mind 21
We Are Joint Heirs with Christ 22
United with the Lord through Jesus................................... 23
We Are Sanctified in Christ 24
We Are Saints.. 25
We Are Hidden with Christ in God 26
We Are Holy and Share in God's Heavenly Calling 27
Firmly Rooted and Built up in Christ 28
Born of God and Kept by Jesus.. 29
We Have the Mind of Christ 30
Approach God with Boldness, Freedom, and Confidence 32
We Are Made Complete in Christ....................................... 33

Walking Each Day with Him in His Love 35
Direct Access to God 36
Assured All Things Are Working Together for Good 37

Free from Condemning Charges	38
Deeply Rooted in Him	39
Established, Anointed, and Sealed by God	40
God Will Complete the Good Work He Started in Us	41
God Brings Light and Life to the Darkest Places	42
Our Refuge and Strength	43
Our Strong Tower	44
His Love Endures Forever	45
Perfect Love Casts Out Fear	46
The Bread of Life	47
Living Water	48
The Gate	49
The Lord Hears our Heart's Cry	50
Stand Still in His Peace	51
Our Defender	52
Nothing Can Suppress the Power of God	53
Prince of Peace	55
The Good Shepherd	56
The First Noel	57
Rejoice! Unto Us, a Savior Is Born	58
El Roi: The God Who Sees Me	59
The Great "I Am"	60
Seek First His Kingdom	61
Fellowship with the Lord	62
God Is Light	63
Set Apart	64
Be Still and Wait	65
Living in Love for Others	66
Present Your Requests before God	67
Pressing Onward	69
Christlike Humility	70
Offense Separates, but Love Conquers	71
Love	72
Love Is Patient	73
Love Is Kind	74
Love Does Not Envy	75
Love Does Not Boast	76
Love Is Not Rude or Self-Seeking	77
Love Is Not Easily Angered	78
Love Keeps No Record of Wrongs	79
Love Does Not Delight in Evil	80
Love Always Protects	81
Love Always Trusts	82
Love Always Hopes	83

Love Always Perseveres	84
Love Never Fails	85
Seek the Lord	86
Wise in Heart	87
Get Wisdom and Guard Your Heart	88
The Tongue Has the Power of Life or Death	89
Foster Love in Love for Others	90
The Lord Establishes Your Plans and Steps	91
Be Humble	92
Loving God Enables Us to Love Others	93
The Lord God Will Keep You	94
God Will Uphold Us	95
Train for a Crown that Lasts Forever	97
Keep in Step with the Spirit	98
I Bow My Knees to the Father	99
Ask the Father to Teach You to Fast and Pray	100
Prayer and Fasting in Your Secret Place	101
Bear One Another's Burdens	102
Anticipate the Victory	103
Seeing Others through God's Eyes	104
Seeing Circumstances through God's Eyes	105
Abide in Christ	106
Rejoice, Be Patient, and Pray	107
Let Your Life Be a Testimony	108
The Life of Jesus in Us	109
Search Me, Oh God	110
His Word Is Written on Your Heart	111
You Are His Special Treasure	112
Be Wise with Your Time	113
Sound Your Trumpet	114
Stand on the Anchor	115
Healing Starts within Our Hearts	116
Wake Up! Don't Drift Off to Sleep	117
The Importance of Fellowship	118
A Daily Walk	119
Rest in the Lord	120
Be Separate	121
Walk His Way	122
Enjoy His Journey for You	123
Build Your House on the Rock	124
Pray The Lord Sends Laborers into His Harvest	125
We Are Laborers Together with God	126
God Brings the Harvest	127

Go! The Time Is Now	128
Hope	129
Our hope is in the Lord	130
Persevere in Hope	131
Our Hope and Help	132
Standing and Suffering for Christ	133
Look Up, Press In, and Press On	134
Abound in Hope	135
God Keeps Our Peace	136
Give Thanks and Live Wisely	137
Be Reconciled to God	138
God Equips You as He Calls You	139
Rend Your Heart Unto the Lord	140
God Will Speak to You—Listen	141
Ever Asked God "Why?"	142
Walk by Faith	143
Not by Sight	144
The Lord Weighs the Heart	145
True Freedom	146
Obedience Brings Blessing	147
God Can Give One Step at a Time	148
You Are Needed in the Body of Christ	149
We Are Called to Share the Gospel Message	150
Commissioned for His Mission	151
Wait, Receive, and Then Go	152
His LIFE through You	153
Christlike Character	154
Purified Like Silver	155
Trained by the Master Vinedresser	156
Make Me Your Vessel	157
Produce Christlike Fruit through Me	158

Living for His Glory

Is there a desire in your heart to live your life with heavenly, supernatural purpose and power? God is ready to help you! *Living for His glory is a supernatural choice. It is a desire that wells up in our hearts and souls by His Spirit.*

"Therefore, whether you eat or drink, or whatever you do, do all to the glory of God" **(1 Cor. 10:31 NKJV).**

How do you start (or continue)? *Surrender.* Surrender your life to Him, surrender all your plans to Him, and surrender all you think you are to Him. His way is so much greater! It is so much sweeter, and God will accomplish more through you than you could ever imagine on your own.

Believe in who He is and who He is within you! The power of God dwells within those who believe.

"But you are not in the flesh but in the Spirit, if indeed the Spirit of God dwells in you. Now if anyone does not have the Spirit of Christ, he is not His. And if Christ is in you, the body is dead because of sin, but the Spirit is life because of righteousness" **(Rom. 8:9–10).**

Commune with your heavenly Father so He can speak to you, mold and shape you, and equip you for all He wants to do through you. *You* are His plan to spread the gospel message to this generation!

Choose to ask the Lord for His plan and for His equipping to walk in it. He will always equip you for all He wants to do through you.

I can testify that if I had focused only on what I wanted to be when I grew up as a child, I might have been a veterinarian or a marine biologist (both wonderful things that God can use for His glory if it is His will). However, God's plan is so much better! I'm a daughter of the most high King, empowered by His Holy Spirit. He equipped me to be His light for His glory as a wife, mother of many, walking miracle healed from Stage 4 cancer, teacher of His Word, lover of others through food and clothing ministry, administrator for Him, worship leader, piano player and teacher, corporate leader, small business owner, and recently, an author. I am nothing in my own strength, and some in the secular world may even discount me, but I'm beloved in my heavenly Father's eyes. You are too.

I would never have fathomed any of it. It is only by His grace, and it is all always for His glory! His way has been so much greater than I could ever imagine on my own. I don't know all that His future will bring, but I'm humbly excited for His next adventure.

Friends, this collection of devotionals is a reflection of personal communion and time with Him. I'm honored to joyfully share it with you. I pray for life-changing, supernatural equipping as He fans the flame of your heart's desire to live for His glory.

Remember to reference your three personal questions listed in the preface and on the back cover of the book and talk to Him about them for each devotional.

Once you answer your three questions, move on to the next devotional.

Questions are listed in the preface and the back cover of this book.

Start today by reading the scriptures within the context of His Word in this devotional and talking to Him.

Let's live for Him and all for His glory!

> **LIVING FOR HIS GLORY**
>
> God created us to live for His purpose and Glory.
>
> 1 Corinthians 10:31 "Therefore, whether you eat or drink, or whatever you do, do all to the glory of God."
>
> Colossians 3:17, 23-24 "¹⁷And whatever you do in word or deed, do all in the name of the Lord Jesus, giving thanks to God the Father through Him." "²³And whatever you do, do it heartily, as to the Lord and not to men," "²⁴Knowing that from the Lord you will receive the reward of the inheritance; for you serve the Lord Christ."
>
> Let's choose to live for His Glory and press onward to His High Calling!
>
> Philippians 3:14 "I press onward toward the goal for the prize of the upward call of God in Christ Jesus."
>
> Surrender, BELIEVE, Choose Him, Commune.

Who Are We in God?

I Have Access to God's Wisdom

The Lord's wisdom in us starts with *belief*—belief in who God is; who His Son, Jesus, is; what He did on the cross for the sake of our salvation; and who He is in us, by His Spirit. He has given us the most wonderful instruction manual—the precious Word of God. He has given us His Holy Spirit, who lives in us and teaches us as we yield to Him. Thank you, Lord!

This does require something of us. Yes, it starts with believing, but God's Word says if you lack wisdom, *ask* for it **(See James 1:5)**. Have you ever tried to become friends with someone, really start a relationship and friendship? It takes *effort*. You have to try to get to know the other person and learn about their family, favorite food, activities, etc. You can't expect to be friends with someone you haven't taken the time to get to know and shown your interest in. Make sense?

It's no different with our God, our Creator, mighty King of Kings, yet He is ready to be our loving friend. Will you sit down and commune with Him today? His Word says He is ready to give generously to you.

Believe. Ask. Seek. Knock. He's already sitting at the table, friend.

Note: Remember to follow the instructions outlined in the preface.

When you can answer the three personal questions, you are ready to move to the next devotional.

> **I Have Access to Gods Wisdom**
>
> James 1:5-8 "If any of you lacks wisdom, you should ask God, who gives generously to all without finding fault, and it will be given to you. ⁶But when you ask, you must believe and not doubt, because the one who doubts is like a wave of the sea, blown and tossed by the wind. That person should not expect to receive anything from the Lord. ⁸Such a person is double-minded and unstable in all they do."
>
> Matthew 7:7 "Ask and it will be given to you; seek and you will find; knock and the door will be opened to you."

The Holy Spirit Lives in Me

I'm asking the Lord to help me live a life of *active* faith! As I pray about the upcoming year, I'm praying for His direction, to build up and encourage others in His way, and for Him to be glorified in amazing ways I could never imagine.

Does that desire burn in your heart?

If yes, tell the Lord about it and thank Him! If your honest response is, "Darlene, I just don't feel that desire, but I want to," thank you for being honest! Tell Him that too. *Believe* in who He *is*, not in how you feel. God's Word says that He *wants* us to know the *exceeding greatness of His power toward* us who *believe.* That power is the same as the mighty power exerted when He raised Christ from the dead! Think about that! The same great power that God used to raise Christ from the dead is the same power that lives in YOU and me by His Spirit **(*See* Eph. 1:17–20).**

Pray with me: *Oh Lord, help me to believe in your glorious ways and to be obedient to Your voice. Help me to believe, Lord, that because your Spirit lives in me, You will move through my life as I believe, listen, and obey. You, Lord, know the plan You have for me, and it is the most perfect way. Amen.*

> **The Holy Spirit Lives In ME!**
>
> I Cor. 3:16 "Do you not know that you are the temple of God and that the Spirit of God dwells in you?"
>
> Eph 1:17-20 "...that the God of our Lord Jesus Christ, the Father of glory, may give to you the spirit of wisdom and revelation in the knowledge of Him, ¹⁸the eyes of your understanding being enlightened; that you may know what is the hope of His calling, what are the riches of the glory of His inheritance in the saints, ¹⁹and what is the exceeding greatness of His power toward us who BELIEVE, according to the working of His Mighty Power ²⁰which He worked in Christ when He raised Him from the dead and seated Him at His right hand in the heavenly places...."

I Am Helped by God

Psalm 84:11 says, "For the Lord God *is* a sun and shield; / The Lord will give grace and glory; / No good *thing* will He withhold / From those who walk uprightly."

I just love this description of God. He is a *sun* and *shield.* The sun gives light, brings warmth, and encourages *life.* It also, at its surface, is so hot that we as humans could never physically touch it; we could never get close to it. Not so with our Lord God. He wants us to be close to Him. With this picture in mind, think about how He shields us. He is our guard and protector in all things (no matter the heat) as we rely on Him.

What a *promise* He gives us—a promise of grace, mercy, and love. He is our hiding place, our refuge, and our ever-present help.

We are helped by God! We just have to *ask, listen,* and *obey*. Choose to trust Him and to ask for His help in all things.

Pray with me: *Thank you, Lord, that in* all *circumstances, no matter what, You never leave or forsake us. We are helped by You. Help me, by Your Holy Spirt, to remember to ask for Your help in all things. Amen.*

> I AM HELPED BY GOD
>
> Hebrews 4:16 "Let us therefore come boldly to the throne of grace, that we may obtain mercy and find grace to help in time of need."
>
> Psalms 46:1 "God is our REFUGE and STRENGTH, a very present help in trouble."
>
> Psalms 84:11 "For the Lord God is a sun and shield; The Lord will give grace and glory; no good thing will He withhold from those who walk uprightly."
>
> I choose to trust You God, and to ask for Your help.

I Am Reconciled to God

It is the truth that we are reconciled to God through Christ Jesus the moment we ask Him to be our Savior and Lord of our lives. We are called to represent Christ as His ambassadors. The Greek root of reconciliation is *katallage'* (kat-al-lag-ay') in *Strong's Concordance*; it means "exchange or adjustment of difference, reconciliation, or restoration to favor." We are reconciled to God as a result of Jesus exchanging His righteousness through death on the cross for our sins.

Second Corinthians 5:20–21 says, "Now then, we are ambassadors for Christ, as though God were pleading through us: we implore you on Christ's behalf, be reconciled to God. For He made Him who knew no sin *to be* sin for us, that we might become the righteousness of God in Him."

Let's pray: *Lord God, thank you that we are reconciled to You through Your Son, Jesus. Help us, Lord, to be Your ambassadors.*

> **I Am Reconciled to God**
>
> Romans 5:11 "And not only that, but we also rejoice in God through our Lord Jesus Christ, through whom we have now received the reconciliation."
>
> 2 Cor. 5:18-20 "Now all things are of God, who has reconciled us to Himself through Christ Jesus, and has given us the ministry of reconciliation, that is, that God was in Christ reconciling the world to Himself, not imputing their trespasses to them, and has committed to us the word of reconciliation. ²⁰Now then, we are ambassadors for Christ, as though God were pleading through us: we implore you on Christ's behalf, be reconciled to God."

I Am Tenderly Loved by God

God's Word says He *loves* us with an everlasting love. I love that. No matter where my heart is at, He loves me (you) with an everlasting love! He is just waiting to commune with you.

It starts with *believing* and a *pure* heart.

You might be thinking, "What is up with this word, *believe*?" Well, it is not just some popular word meant for bumper stickers, wall art, and bookmarks.

Let me put it this way: You either *believe*, or you don't. There is no in-between. It's that simple.

Your life communing with our heavenly Father starts here! Believing in who God is, believing that He gave His only Son, Jesus, who died on the cross for our sins to give us everlasting life, and believing in the power of the Holy Spirit who lives in us. You have to *believe* this.

Our Father wants us to have *pure* hearts before Him. We are a mess. I'm a mess! The good news is that God always knew this, and it is why He gave us Jesus! Thank you, Lord.

Go sit at the table with Him, confess your mess, and approach Him with a pure heart. He's waiting for you, and He tenderly, generously *loves* you! He has plans for you, by the way.

Will you pray with me? *Father God, help me to stand on and walk in Your precious promises, to live a life of knowing who You are fully, without hindrance. Help me to live a life that brings You glory by Your power through me, God. Make it so real to my heart, God, just how much You tenderly love me so that I may share Your love with others. Amen.*

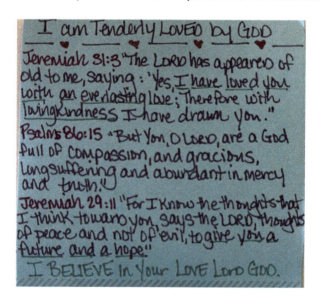

We Are Children of God

John 1:12–13 says "But as many as received Him, to them He gave the right to become children of God, to those who believe in His name: who were born, not of blood, nor of the will of the flesh, nor of the will of man, but of God"

We are His precious sons and daughters. We are part of His glorious kingdom. We are given mercy, and we are made to declare the praises of Him who calls us out of darkness and into the truth of who He is.

We are not our own. We are *not* our *own*. The flesh doesn't like to hear this. We are here on this earth for His purpose. Do you believe that about yourself? I lived so many years trying to do my best to accomplish all the things the world says we should and please others. Thank you, Lord, for opening my eyes to have a desire to only do what You call me to do and to only do it to please You—all for His glory! Such *freedom*.

My heart rejoices to be His chosen, beloved child, part of a royal priesthood and His holy nation. So are you!

> We are children of God & belong to Him!
>
> **John 1:12** As many as recieved Him, to them He gave the right to become children of God, to those who believe in His name.
>
> **1 Cor 6:19,20** We belong to the Lord! Your body is the temple of the Holy Spirit who is in you, who you have from God, and you are not your own! You were bought at a price, glorify God in body & spirit which are God's.
>
> **1 Peter 2:9** You are A PRINCESS! Prince! You are a chosen people, a Royal priesthood, a holy nation – GOD'S SPECIAL POSSESSION.......

We Are the Sweet Fragrance of Christ to God

When we spend time with our heavenly Father, He leads us according to His plan. As we walk *with* Him, others know it! They can see that something is different about us; His presence goes with us and before us. His presence will completely change the atmosphere of a room. His Word says through us He "diffuses the fragrance of His knowledge in every place" **(2 Cor. 2:14)**.

I've lived it! Working a job in the corporate world as an executive always brought its challenges. Meetings with believers and unbelievers alike, differences of opinion, style, and values brought conflict. There have been those occasions when that one "personality" in the room just takes over. Know what I'm talking about? Maybe it's the loudest most outspoken person who has ideas that are thought to be the only right ones at the time. Or maybe it's the one who really just likes to be heard and has a negative spirit that dampens the whole room? Or maybe it's the one who has an underlying personal goal that may narrow the focus or outcome of what the group is trying to accomplish. How about the one who is quiet and reserved with amazing insight but isn't heard? I've seen it all.

What I can say *never* fails is walking in love in my responses toward others and inviting the presence of God into the room. How? I simply pray and ask for His presence. I invite Him into the room, the conversation, and ask for His wisdom in response. Although done in my mind and heart, the outcome is always the same: God's favor guides the conversation, He changes the atmosphere, and the job gets done. I can look back now and see the favor of God's hand in the workplace and how He used it for His glory and the testament of what others witnessed of God in me.

For His glory, we *are* the sweet fragrance of Christ to God wherever He places our hands and feet.

Let's pray: Lord God, help us to believe in Your love and power and to walk in it so that You can love others through us! You make us to be the sweet-smelling fragrance of Christ. I thank You, God. Amen.

> We are the Sweet Fragrance of Christ to God
>
> 2 Cor. 2:14-15 "Now thanks be to God who always leads us in triumph in Christ and through us diffuses the fragrance of His knowledge in every place. For we are to God the fragrance of Christ among those who are being saved and among those who are perishing."
>
> 1 Peter 4:8 "And above all things have fervent love for one another, for 'love will cover a multitude of sins.'"
>
> Eph 5:2 "And walk in love, as Christ also has loved us and given Himself for us, an offering and a sacrifice to God for a sweet-smelling aroma."

Are God's Living Stones

First Peter 2:5 struck me one morning: "You also, as living stones, are being built up a spiritual house, a holy priesthood, to offer up spiritual sacrifices acceptable to God through Jesus Christ."

Living stones? I'm reminded that in the natural, the supernatural things of the Lord may seem strange or ridiculous to eyes that are blind to His ways. I'm thankful the Lord can use simple, natural expressions like *living stones* to help me understand the power of standing on whom Christ is for us: the Chief Cornerstone.

You know, it wasn't until I was walking through the ruins in Rome once, close to the Colosseum, that I saw at the corner of the foundation of an old ruin an actual cornerstone. The design was pretty amazing as all other stones were strategically placed above and around so that the burden of the structure rested upon it. You could see that in its time, all the stones together made an amazing structure that remains solid to the present day.

What a wonderful picture God gives us. Jesus Christ as our Chief Cornerstone is our first and most solid footing. The Lord wants us to build our very lives upon Him. To live life in Him. Building upon anything else is just shifting sand. I thank God that He does this through His Spirit in us over time. We are His house, each of us a stone built upon the Chief Cornerstone and together, He does amazing things for His kingdom's purpose.

Remember, when you can answer the three personal questions outlined in the preface, you are ready to move to the next devotional.

Let's pray: *Father, help me to believe and to walk in Your ways, to build my life upon who you are and your Word, and to believe I am a temple for Your Spirit. Build us up, Lord. We are Your living stones!*

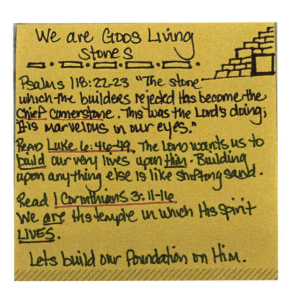

We Are Part of God's Holy Nation

You are God's chosen generation, royal priesthood, a holy nation, *His own special people* **(1 Peter 2:9–10** my emphasis**).**

When we believe and receive who Jesus Christ is for us with a humble and repentant heart, we become part of God's holy nation. We are His.

Satan cannot snatch you out of God's hand. As you choose to set in your heart to be set apart for God, nothing can separate you from His love. Let's be honest and clear: you can choose to walk away from God, who is always there waiting for you to turn back and look to Him. However, for the hearts set on Him, *nothing*—*no thing,* no physical entity—can separate them from God's love.

"For I am persuaded that neither death nor life, nor angels nor principalities nor powers, nor things present nor things to come, nor height nor depth, nor any other created thing, shall be able to separate us from the love of God which is in Christ Jesus our Lord." **(Rom. 8:38–39)**

> We are Part of God's Holy Nation
> 1 Peter 2:9-10 "But you are a chosen generation, a royal priesthood, a holy nation, His own special people, that you may proclaim the praises of Him who called you out of darkness into His marvelous light; ¹⁰who once were not a people but are now the people of God, who had not obtained mercy but now have obtained mercy."

We Are the Salt of the Earth

Matthew 5:13 says, "You are the salt of the earth; but if the salt loses its flavor, how shall it be seasoned? It is then good for nothing but to be thrown out and trampled underfoot by men."

In the Hebrew society of the Old Testament, salt was used as a seasoning, preservative, disinfectant, and in sacrifices.

When Jesus said this in Matthew, to the people of that time, the salt metaphor was very relatable. Today, we may have to think about it a bit more. He was saying that as a believer with the knowledge of God our King and the saving grace of Jesus Christ, you bring the *seasoning of life* to others. It will *preserve* you. The knowledge and saving grace that Christ's forgiveness brings will *cleanse* you. When you share it with other believers, the truth of His Word can sting a bit on old sinful wounds, but it will bring *healing* to those who choose to believe the gospel message.

God's Word also says that we are salted with *fire* by His Spirit! **(Mark 9:49–50 ESV)**

I don't know about you, but I want to be salty! If we, as believers, choose not to commune with our Father, if we slowly walk away from our relationship with Him, we lose our saltiness. We are unable to share by the power of His Holy Spirit if we choose not to walk in it.

Let's ask for His help: *Father, I need you. I want to be the salt of the earth for You. I realize I cannot do this without the help of Your Spirit. Put Your Word in my heart and on my tongue so that it may be shared and be salt for the sake of salvation and for Your glory. Thank you, Lord. Amen.*

> **We are the Salt of the Earth**
> —*—*—
> As believers, we are salted with FIRE by the Holy Spirit.
> Mark 9: 49-50 "For everyone will be seasoned with FIRE, and every sacrifice will be seasoned with salt. ⁵⁰Salt is good, but if the salt loses its flavor, how will you season it? Have salt in yourselves, and have peace with one another."
> By God's grace we can walk through each day in All He calls us to, seasoned as salt and ready to respond to others.
> Colossians 4:6 "Let your speech always be with grace, seasoned with salt, that you may know how you ought to answer each one."

We Are Light in This World

We are both salt and light in this world.

Read **John 8:12 NKJV** where Jesus says, "I am the light of the world. He who follows Me shall not walk in darkness but have the light of life."

Now read **1 John 1:5–9**. Within the text, it shares that "God is light and in Him there is no darkness at all." As we fellowship and commune with God with pure hearts and walk *with* Him, we also walk in His light because of the gift of Christ Jesus.

His light in us exposes sin and brings the light of life through Christ Jesus everywhere He sends us—*everywhere* He sends us—home, work, the grocery store, the gas station—*everywhere*. I'm reminded not to discount His light in me wherever I go. Without a word, others can see that a life lived for Christ is different. His light cannot be hidden!

Pray with me: *Oh Lord, thank you for making me salt and light everywhere You send my hands and feet. Help me to be bold and obedient in Your ways. Amen.*

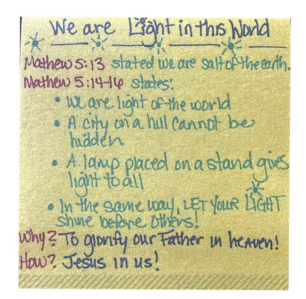

My Needs Are Met by God

"And my God shall supply all your need according to His riches in glory by Christ Jesus." **(Phil. 4:19)**

Our Father knows our needs before we even *ask* Him. He sees us in every moment. There is a keyword though: *ask*. We have to choose to take action and ask Him for our needs in the name of Jesus. The Lord wants us to *believe* Him, *trust* Him, and move and walk *in obedience*. Our part is to *look* to Him, *ask* Him with a thankful heart, and then *rest* in Him while we *wait* on Him. Even if His response isn't what you envisioned it to be, trust He is always for your good.

Let's pray: *Above all else, all I need is You, Lord. You are the faithful, true, and mighty King—omnipotent and omnipresent—You are the One who knows the intent of the heart and the reasons we cry out to You. Thank you, Lord, for always hearing our hearts' cry. Amen.*

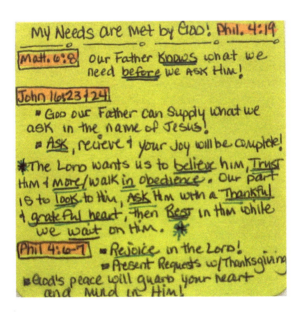

Great and Precious Promises of God

As His divine power has given to us all things that pertain to life and godliness, through the knowledge of Him who called us by glory and virtue, by which have been given to us exceedingly great and precious promises, that through these you may be partakers of the divine nature, having escaped the corruption that is in the world through lust. **(2 Peter 1:3–4)**

Our Father's promises to us are infinite, rock solid, and completely unmovable. His promises are "Yes" and "Amen." Nothing—*no thing,* no physical entity—can separate us from Him. He goes with us and never leaves us.

How will you walk in this today? Where or when do you need help standing in His promise?

Read the context of the scriptures given and talk to Him about it.

Who Is Christ in Us?

The Way, the Truth, and the Life

"Jesus answered 'I am the way, the truth, and the life. No one comes to the Father except through Me'" **(John 14:6 New International Version).**

I was thinking one day about how overwhelming circumstances can be at times. I have to protect my time with our Father, maintain time with my husband, and balance time with family; meanwhile, Mom is fighting cancer, Dad has overall health concerns, and work can be stressful and demanding. I am abandoned to His ministry twenty-four seven, which means long days and little sleep in a sin-sick world.

Sometimes, overwhelming circumstances are our own, and other times, we are impacted by someone else's overwhelming circumstances. Maybe we are standing in prayer for others for the loss of a loved one, sickness, substance abuse, or rejection and hurt from a relative, close friend, or even someone they barely know! The list is endless.

I found myself just thinking, "In the midst of all this mess, Lord, all my hope is in You! It's way too much to bear; so, Lord, I'm laying it all back down at Your feet. You are the only way, You are pure truth, and by the work You did on the cross, You bring everlasting life! Help me, Lord, to lay everything at Your feet each day. I choose to rest in You."

Is there anything you need to lay at His feet today? Talk to Him. Let's walk each day and believe this together.

> Jesus is the way, Truth, and the Life!
> John 14:6 Jesus answered "I am the way, the Truth and the Life. No one comes to the Father except through me."
> THE WAY: The door, the gate, THE mediator
> 1 Timothy 2:5 "For there is one God and mediator between God and man, the man Christ Jesus!"
> The TRUTH: Undeniable fact or reality
> John 8:31-32 "Jesus said, If you hold to my teaching, you are my disciples. Then you will know the truth, and the truth will set you free."
> The LIFE: Eternal, everlasting LIFE!
> Acts 4:12 "Salvation is found in no one else, for there is no other name under heaven given to mankind by which we must be saved."

We Are Branches on Christ's Vine

Read **John 15:1–5**. God our Father is our Vinedresser or Master Gardener. He cares for, cultivates, and prunes our lives.

Think about what *cultivate* means. Look up the definition in a few different dictionaries; different descriptions can bring fresh revelation to our hearts. When you cultivate land, you are turning soil over, helping it to be as ready and fertile as possible, protecting it from weeds and bugs. Think about the process of *pruning* (trimming off dead branches or overgrowth to increase fruitfulness). Feel free to look this up as well.

This process of cultivating and pruning isn't always pleasant in our lives, but it will always bear His intended fruit as we walk with Him.

Jesus is the vine, and we are the branches. *We should bear fruit!*

Our God loves us so much that He cultivates us, He cuts off unfruitful branches, and He prunes the fruitful ones in our lives.

Let's thank Him: *Lord, I thank You for carefully watching over me. For being the Master Gardener of my life. Thank You for caring for and watching over me as I grow in You. You are the cultivator of my heart and life. Make me fruitful for Your glory, Lord, and I thank You for the work. Thank You for Your Son, Jesus, who makes the way for us to be free and forgiven. Thank You for Your Holy Spirit, who trains, teaches, and guides us in all Your ways. Amen.*

Remember to talk to Him about your three personal questions.

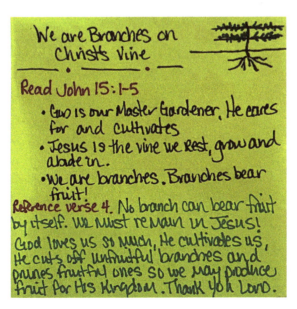

The Indwelling and Outpouring of the Holy Spirit

As believers, we have the indwelling Holy Spirit who takes up residence in us the moment we choose to admit we are sinners and accept Christ Jesus as our Lord and Savior. The evidence of the Holy Spirit is seen in our lives and the lives of other believers by the fruit of the Holy Spirit. Read **Galatians 5:22–24**.

But there is *more*. Yes, more. We can also walk in an outpouring of His Holy Spirit, which is evident through manifested gifts of the Holy Spirit.

I invite you to dive into the context of all reference scriptures and commune with our Lord about them. Don't forget to answer all of your personal questions before moving on to the next devotional. You may be on this one for a while!

Let's pray: *Lord help me to believe Your truth and to walk in the fullness of who You are with all that I am. Do something new in my heart. Teach me in a fresh way how to walk by Your Spirit. All for Your glory, Lord. Amen.*

I Have the _Indwelling_ Holy Spirit and can walk in the _outpouring_ of His Spirit!

INDWELLING Spirit

Eph 1:13-14
- You were _included_ in Christ when you heard and accepted Truth.
- You were _marked_ in Him with a seal by the _promised_ Holy _Spirit_ when you _believed_.
- The Holy Spirit is a _deposit_.

John 14:15-17 If you love me keep my commands (believe) v.17 The Holy Spirit lives _IN_ and _with_ you. (indwelling)

1 Cor. 12:31 _Earnestly_ desire the BEST gifts and I'll show you the most excellent way.... LOVE!

Through the promised Holy Spirit, we can walk in the best gifts to LOVE others and Glorify God.

Outpouring of His Spirit

Luke 11:11-13 ... how much more will your Father in heaven give the Holy Spirit to those that ask?

1 Cor. 14:1 Follow the way of LOVE and eagerly desire the gifts of the Spirit.

Eph 5:18-19 ... Be _filled_ with the Spirit!

Acts 1:8 ... You will receive power when the Spirit comes _UPON_ you!

Acts 2:15-21 v.17 "I will POUR OUT my Spirit on _all_ people (believers). v.18 Both man and woman — on His servants."

Why? In LOVE FOR OTHERS. For Salvation for the unbeliever.
v.21 and everyone who calls on the name of the Lord will be SAVED!

Jesus Is Our Friend

Isn't it overwhelming, the breadth of who God our Father and His Son, Jesus, are to us? God, our Creator and mighty King of Kings, sovereign over all forever and ever. His Son, in His Majesty, gives us the opportunity for everlasting life. Just thinking of it draws me to my knees in reverence. Yet, *He is also simply our friend*.

We are reminded of this in the life of Abraham. He was considered righteous in the eyes of God. Why? Because he *believed* in God's word to him **(Gen. 15:5–6)**.

We later can see his life testament in this scripture: "And the Scripture was fulfilled which says, 'Abraham believed God, and it was accounted to him for righteousness.' And he was called the friend of God" **(James 2:23 NKJV)**.

Read **John 15:13–15**. We *are* His friends if we do what He commands. What does He command us to do? To love Him with all our heart, mind, and soul and to love one another.

We also need one another as friends of Christ within the body of Christ. We sharpen one another **(**See **Proverbs 27:17)**!

> **Jesus Is Our Friend**
>
> Read John 15:13-15
> - We are His friend if we believe and do what He commands
> - He calls us friends for everything
> - Christ learned from His Father, He has made known to us.
>
> We need each other as friends of Christ within the body of Christ.
>
> Proverbs 27:17 "Iron sharpens iron, so one man sharpens another."

A Spirit of Power, Love, and a Sound Mind

"For God has not given us a spirit of fear, but of *power* and of *love* and of a *sound mind*" **(2 Timothy 1:7 emphasis added).**

The *moment* we accept Christ into our hearts, His Holy Spirit takes up residence in us. I think we, at times, can forget the immeasurable source of strength that lives within us. Have you ever had those days when everything on the outside and around you is seemingly at peace, but internally, you are *fighting*? Have you found yourself fighting thoughts of fear, doubt, and indecision that are constantly distracting you in your prayer and communion time with Him?

I know; I have been there. This fighting ground is the Lord's! The fiery darts of the enemy hitting our thought lives have no power—unless we let them. Satan gets no credit in my heart, but his goal is to distract us and take our eyes off our Lord. We are called to fight by His Spirit and stand on His promise in **2 Timothy 1:7**. How?

"Therefore, submit to God. Resist the devil and he will flee from you. Draw near to God and He will draw near to you" **(James 4:7–8).**

Submit, resist, draw near; then, thank Him for the victory He has already won through Christ Jesus.

Dive into the context of scripture to meditate on the fullness of the words *power*, *love*, and *mind* in **2 Timothy 1:7.**

Remember, when you can answer the three personal questions outlined in the preface, you are ready to move to the next devotional.

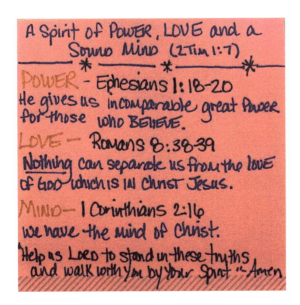

We Are Joint Heirs with Christ

I love the promise God gives us as captured in **Romans 8**. We are children of our sovereign God and, as a result, co-heirs with Christ. In what? *Everlasting life* in His heavenly kingdom *forever*.

Why the word *heir*? We *inherit* this gift as His children.

This inheritance can never spoil, perish, or fade (*See* **1 Peter 1:3–4**).

When I think about all that God has done for us, how He gave us His Son, Jesus, and sent Him to the cross to cleanse the world of sin, it brings joy to my heart. Think on that. Thank Him. We have everlasting life! Go ahead and *rejoice*!

No other investment plan can ever give that. I choose to invest in Jesus!

> We are Joint heirs with Christ!
>
> **Romans 8:17** Now if we are children, then we are heirs – heirs of God and co-heirs with Christ, if indeed we share in His sufferings, in order that we may also share in His Glory!
>
> **1 Peter 1:3-4** In His Mercy He has given us a new birth into a living hope through the ressurection of Jesus!.... and into an inheritance that can never perish, never spoil, never fade!
>
> **Matthew 25:34** Then the King will say, "come you who are blessed by My Father; take your inheritance, the KINGDOM, prepared for you since the creation of the World!

United with the Lord through Jesus

Because of Christ Jesus, who is the way to our Father, we are united or joined with the Lord.

First Corinthians 6:17 states, "But he who is joined to the Lord is one spirit *with Him*."

What does it mean for us to have unity with God? It means we can have *a direct relationship*, commune with Him directly, and hear from Him by His Spirit. Thank you, Lord!

Did you know that Jesus prayed to our Holy Father for this? Read **John 17:20–23**.

What *love* for us! The heart of Jesus when He prayed this to His Father was for us to be brought into complete unity with God our Father. Why? Always for the glory of God, so that the world may know that God sent Jesus for the sake of salvation for the world.

We are His witnesses.

> United with the Lord Through Jesus
> Did you know? Jesus prayed to our Holy Father, for all who will believe in Him, that we will all be one with Him.
> John 17:20-23 "I do not pray for these alone, but also for those who will believe in Me through their word; that they all may be one, as You, Father are in Me, and I in You; that they also may be one in Us, that the world may believe that You sent Me. ²²And the glory which You gave Me I have given them, that they may be one just as We are one: ²³I in them, and You in Me; that they may be made perfect in one, and that the world may know that You have sent Me, and I have loved them as You have loved Me."

We Are Sanctified in Christ

Let's rejoice in our Savior's gift to us! In devotionals up to this point, we have looked at scripture about who we are in God and who Christ is in us. We have reminded ourselves of the *inheritance* we have through Jesus, how we are *reconciled* through Him, *united* with Him, and *justified* by Him. We are also *sanctified* by the gift of His Spirit who lives in us!

I don't know about you, but even though I've studied and read His Word for over thirty years and learned about each of the words emphasized above, understanding the true meaning of each when compared to one another still further deepens my personal knowledge of Him. I like to call this gaining a little head knowledge for the greater purpose of heart understanding. Go ahead, look back on some of the prior devotionals and compare meanings if helpful.

To be sanctified means to be cleansed or purified from our sins, to be set apart or declared holy (*The KJV Dictionary*). Sanctification is the work of the spirit of Christ in us helping us to walk through life for Him in the holiness of Christ. I believe we are sanctified the moment we accept Christ as our Savior and forgiven of all sin, *and* that it is a continuous process of refinement in our hearts and characters as our Father refines us to make us more like Him over time.

Let us pray: *Oh Lord, my heart just yearns for more of You! Continue to purify my heart and my character and to make me more Christlike for Your eternal purpose, kingdom, and glory, Lord!*

> We are Sanctified in Christ
>
> Hebrews 2:10-11 "For it was fitting for Him, for whom are all things and by whom are all things, in bringing many sons to glory, to make the captain of their salvation perfect through sufferings. For both He who sanctifies and those who are being sanctified are all of one, for which reason He is not ashamed to call them brethren...."
>
> • God made Jesus, the pioneer of our salvation and sanctification perfect through the work on the cross.
> • Through His death, resurrection and by His spirit we are cleansed, set apart and made holy. He calls us friend.

We Are Saints

Have you ever thought about how you are a saint? I'm sure all kinds of thoughts are going through your mind. You might be thinking, *Darlene, I sure don't feel like a saint* or *Isn't a saint something you call a "super Christian"*? Nope! It is a description given to the body of Christ, those who faithfully believe in Christ Jesus and the precious work He did on the cross for us are His saints. It is not based on how we feel or how perfectly we think we may live our lives for God. We know we are imperfect people, and it's why we need Christ.

The word *saint* comes from the Greek word *hagios* which means "consecrated to God, holy, sacred, or pious" (*Strong's Concordance*). It is almost always used in plural form.

The idea of the word *saints* is a group of people set apart for the Lord and His kingdom. Want to be a saint now?

Reference the scriptures provided below. Explore His Word in the books of Ephesians and Romans and stand in this promise with me.

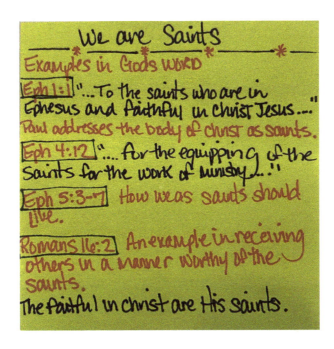

We are Saints
Examples in Gods word
Eph 1:1 "...To the saints who are in Ephesus and faithful in Christ Jesus..."
Paul addresses the body of christ as saints.
Eph 4:12 "...for the equipping of the saints for the work of ministry..."
Eph 5:3-7 How we as saints should live.
Romans 16:2 An example in receiving others in a manner worthy of the saints.
The faithful in christ are His saints.

We Are Hidden with Christ in God

"For you died, and your life is hidden with Christ in God" **(Col. 3:3)**.

"Hidden with" refers to a life lived in Christ, dead to sin; it is abiding in Christ in the midst of the sin-sick world in which we live.

Dive into a few examples of hiding and abiding in Him in both the Old and New Testaments. Let Him speak something fresh to your heart.

Let's pray: *I praise You, Lord! When we choose to live a life in You, You cover us and hide us in You. Your peace is everlasting when we abide in You. Help us in this each new day.*

> We are Hidden with Christ in God
> Examples of Hiding and abiding in God:
> OLD Testament
> Psalms 91:1-2 Dwell in the secret place of the Most high.
> Exodus 33:22 God covers Moses with His hand.
> New Testament
> Romans 6:2 We die to sin
> John 15:4 Abide in Christ
> 2 Cor. 5:7 Walk by faith with Christ

We Are Holy and Share in God's Heavenly Calling

"Therefore, holy brethren, partakers of the heavenly calling, consider the Apostle and High Priest of our confession, Christ Jesus." **(Heb. 3:1)**

We are considered holy by God's amazing grace, created for a heavenly calling for the glory of God's kingdom and for His own purpose. We can never be holy by our works—only by His grace **(2 Tim. 1:9)**. We are created to love Him and share the gospel message of Christ Jesus. The daily walk in this isn't always easy; we will both rejoice and suffer through it all. But it is so *worth* it!

Believe and receive this in your heart in all its fullness.

By grace, we are saved and are given eternal life in heaven. Until then, let's rest in Him in heavenly places by abiding in Him. Christ is the Son over God's house, and *we are His house!*

Read context in **Hebrews**, **2 Timothy**, **Romans**, and **Ephesians**.

Let's pray: *Lord, go before us. Help us to believe who we are through Your grace and Spirit. Help us to believe that Your great power by Your Spirit lives in us. Help us to believe that we are holy through Your grace and that we share in Your heavenly calling. Help us, Lord, to live this as we abide in You.*

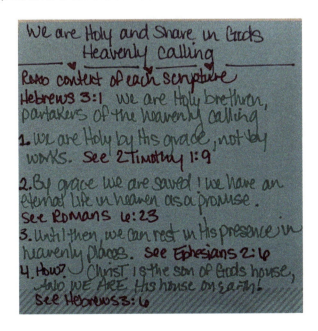

Firmly Rooted and Built Up in Christ

The enemy will try anything to deceive us or distract us with deceptive philosophies and ways of the world. *Do not fear.* Stand in Christ, our solid rock. Read **Matthew 7:24–25.**

I don't know about you, but in our current world with an "anything goes" culture telling us to be who we want to be and do what we want to do or be rejected by what seems to be the mainstream, I need reminding sometimes to stand in Christ.

I am a living testament of His rest and peace in Him—yes, even when others don't like that I'm different for Him.

Read **Colossians 2:6–10**: it's amazing direction with amazing promise.

He strengthens us deeply as He continues to build us up as fortified houses for Him. Whether we are on the mountaintop, in the valley, or in the midst of a chaotic storm, He is there and is faithful to give us the strength needed to be rooted in Him as we walk through it.

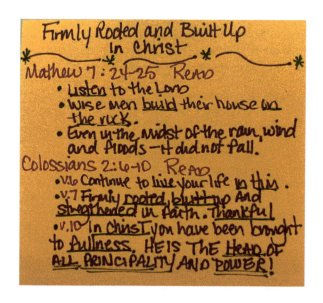

Born of God and Kept by Jesus

Do you believe in God's great power? Do you believe it lives in you?

First John 4:4 says, "You are of God, little children, and have overcome them, because He who is in you is greater than he who is in the world."

I'm comforted and so encouraged by this. Think about this promise! We have the most powerful weapon within us who has already conquered the enemy. We have to walk in this promise as the "whole world lies under the sway of the wicked one" **(1 John 5:19)**.

Whenever I have a challenging circumstance (especially with unbelievers), whether it be in the workplace, at a family function, at the local grocery store, or ministering in the community, I choose to believe in God's great power. I have to *ask* for His help and tap into it! Otherwise, I'm quick to try to do things in my own effort and strength. Sound familiar?

God's Spirit gives us wisdom in difficult circumstances. When I pray and ask the Lord to go before me, He always gives His grace and power for the moment as needed. Always. He has de-escalated angry moments, given wisdom during conflict, provided His eyes to "see" when needed, and offered His amazing grace in the midst of sorrow. Always! It requires us to *believe, ask, listen, obey His voice,* and *step boldly* as He leads, even when it doesn't make sense to our human minds.

You see, the battle was and is never ours; it is the Lord's. He is the one who does all battle in the Spirit. He *equips us* to stand and move in the fight, He makes the armor readily available, and He has already given us the weapon. He is always the Master General, and the *evil one cannot touch us*!

We are born of God, kept by Jesus, and can move in His *great power* by His Spirit. Whether you have known Him for two days or two decades, there is so much more to learn and experience in Him. Thank Him and ask Him to help you understand this more fully today.

> **Born of God and Kept by Jesus**
>
> 1 John 5:18 "We know that whoever is born of God does not sin; but he who has been born of God keeps himself, and the wicked one does not touch him. 19 We know that we are of God, and the whole world lies under the sway of the wicked one."
>
> We are born of God, Kept by Jesus and can move in His Great Power by His Spirit. Thank you for the Victory Lord.
>
> 1 Corinthians 15:57 "But thanks be to God, who gives us the victory through our Lord Jesus Christ."

We Have the Mind of Christ

We are children of God, made new in Him and set apart in this world. By His Spirit who lives in us, we are given a spirit of power, love, and a sound mind—not fear.

You might be thinking, *How?* or *Sometimes, I am afraid.* I totally understand, and I've been there. I am a living testament to God's healing from both sickness and fear. I was diagnosed with Stage 4 ovarian cancer about fourteen years before the date of this writing. Doctors said I had less than a 50 percent chance of living more than six months. Less than 10 percent of ovarian cancer patients had my type of cancer, and the only study they had to reference was from back in the 1980s: a study of twenty women who had already passed away. They told me to write my will.

Just after the shock of the news, fear set in. Fear of what was to come, what treatment and pain I may need to go through, and what my husband would need to go through. Reading online articles and white papers just increased the fear.

I'll never forget the moment, about a week later, when I was on my knees at the altar during a Wednesday night service. A handful of ladies came to pray over me. Right then, in the Spirit, I felt lifted in countenance by God. What may have been a handful of ladies praying at that moment sounded like hundreds to me. In the midst of all of those voices, I heard one that spoke clearly through them all: the Lord simply said, "This sickness is not unto death; I will heal you." I'll never forget this moment. By His Spirit, He anointed me with peace; by His own voice, He spoke a word of promise. True joy entered my heart. I was able to rest in His perfect peace for the next eighteen months of treatment. Seven surgeries later, I still had cancer spots.

It was *after* the eighteen months of chemotherapy and seven surgeries that God healed me in a moment of prayer, touched by His healing hand. Fourteen cancer-free years later, the doctors still call me the miracle patient. God did this in this way for me so that I'd know concretely that it was not by man's hand I was healed but by the hand of God. The journey was a refining training ground for His glory. I have so many testimonies that I'll share in time. Even though it was hard, I would never change it. What God did in my life and the life of my husband is priceless. All glory be to God!

Trust Him.

"Thou wilt keep *him* in perfect peace *whose* mind is stayed on thee: because He trusteth in thee" **(Isa. 26:3 King James Version** emphasis added**).**

> **We have the mind of Christ!**
>
> **1 Cor. 2:16** "Who has known the mind of the Lord so as to instruct him?" But we have the mind of Christ.
>
> **2 Timothy 1:7** For God has not given us a Spirit of fear; but of power, and of love, and of a sound mind.
>
> As believers:
> - ♥ We are His child
> - ♥ We are made new
> - ♥ We are not the same or of this world
> - ♥ We have the mind of Christ, by His Spirit whom lives in us!

Approach God with Boldness, Freedom, and Confidence

Praise be to our Lord whom we can stand firm in and trust all the days of our lives. He asks us to stand firm in Him and to boldly approach Him with confidence!

> Oh, how great *is* Your goodness, / Which You have laid up for those who fear You, / Which You have prepared for those who trust in You / In the presence of the sons of men! / You shall hide them in the secret place of Your presence / From the plots of man; / You shall keep them secretly in a pavilion / From the strife of tongues.
>
> For I said in my haste, / "I am cut off from before Your eyes"; / Nevertheless, You heard the voice of my supplications / When I cried out to you.
>
> Be of good courage, / And He shall strengthen your heart, / All you who hope in the Lord. **(Ps. 31:19–20, 22, 24 NKJV)**

Through Jesus, we can approach the throne of God with confidence. We can have a personal relationship with Him.

Dive into the following scriptures and read the context. May the Lord bless you.
Ephesians 3:12; 2 Corinthians 3:17; John 8:36; and **Hebrews 4:16**

> We can approach God with boldness, freedom and confidence!
> — ✱ — ✱ — ✱ —
> **Eph. 3:12** In Him (Jesus) and through faith in Him, we may approach God with freedom and confidence.
> By His Spirit……
> **2 Cor. 3:17** Now the Lord is the Spirit, and where the Spirit of the Lord is, there is freedom!
> Through the Gift of His Son……
> **John 8:36** So if the Son sets you free, you will be free indeed!
> **Hebrews 4:16** Let us then approach God's throne of grace with confidence, so that we may receive mercy & grace in time of need!

32 | Darlene Harkins

We Are Made Complete in Christ

"Being confident of this very thing, that He who has begun a good work in you will complete it until the day of Jesus Christ" **(Phil. 1:6).**

I am so thankful that the Lord, by His Spirit, is ever changing the hearts and lives of His children. He is always shaping our character and teaching those who are willing to seek and receive. This is a continuous process until the day He takes us to our heavenly home.

He completes His good work in us for the purpose of which He created each of us. It is alwaysfor His glory and so that others may come to the knowledge and saving grace of Christ Jesus.

Read the context of **Colossians 2:1–13** and **Philippians 1:1–11**. Talk to the Lord about your personal questions.

> We are Made COMPLETE IN CHRIST!
> Read Colossians 2:1-13
> v.6 Just as you recieved Christ, continue to live in Him, rooted & built up in strength & overflowing w/ thankfulness.
> v.10 In christ, you have been brought to fullness. He is Head over Every Power and Authority. We are complete in him.
> v.13 When we were dead to our sins, we we were Made alive in Christ!
> Phillippians 1:9-11 A blessing For You
> • May your love abound more & more in knowledge and depth of insight
> • May you discern what is pure & blameless
> • Righteousness comes through Christ.

Walking Each Day with Him in His Love

Direct Access to God

Have you ever thought about how amazing it is that we have *direct access* to God Himself because of the work Jesus did for us on the cross? Yes. *Direct access.*

When I think about a relationship with God, I think about the simple picture of a little table with two chairs. His table is abundant with all things needed. He is always at this table, my chair is pulled back with Him waiting for me to be seated, the conversation is so wonderful as we commune through His Word and prayer. Sometimes, I'm silent, just waiting to hear what He wants to say.

It is so precious, this privilege and gift. Hearing from Him in His presence is the safest place we can be in the midst of a sin-sick world in chaos; yet in that chaotic busyness, it may be the place we spend the least amount of time.

Do you want to change that? If you are reading this and have talked to Him about each of your personal questions for each devotional to this point, you are already on your way! Every time He draws you, come sit at His table in obedience.

Study the context for the scriptures noted and talk to Him about your personal questions.

Let's pray: *Lord, help us and draw us unto You when You call us. Help us to abide in You and spend time with You by coming to sit at Your table to commune with You. Teach us what it means to have a full relationship with You, Lord, so that we are confident in hearing Your voice. You are our ever-present helper, teacher, and friend. Amen.*

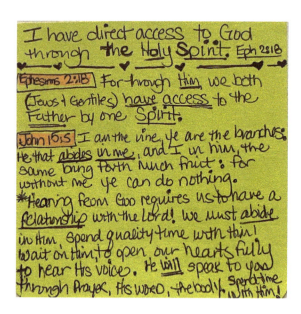

Assured All Things Are Working Together for Good

Our Father is always for our good. Always. For the believer who is pure in heart toward the Lord, every circumstance He allows He can use for His glory. *Every* circumstance: the good, the bad, and the ugly. You see, if you are resting in Him, He knows just how to orchestrate all things in your life for your good—even when they are hard.

He *allowed* me to endure eighteen months of chemo and seven surgeries after being diagnosed with Stage 4 ovarian cancer. He ordained that my husband and I would not be able to have children as a result. The way He cared for my heart through, this was only by His Spirit.

It was *after* all the treatment was complete and with cancer spots still evident in my body that He touched me in a time of prayer and healed me completely. *Completely*. He wanted me to know it wasn't by man's hand I was healed, but by His. The doctors today still call me the miracle patient fourteen years later on this day. I'll say that those eighteen months were *not* wasted. He did so much through that time to draw me to Him, to build faith in my heart in who He is, to teach me in His work, and to draw my husband and me closer together. And through it all, He spoke a word: my sickness wasn't unto death, and even though we were not meant to have children of our own on this earth, He wanted to entrust us with many children by His Spirit. This circumstance was allowed by His hand in my life, and the training was priceless. Now that I see all He did through it, I would never change it.

I used to ask God "Why?" "Why are You allowing this in my life? Are You there?" He taught me through this experience to ask instead, "*What* would *You* like to do, God, through this for Your glory? What would You like to do, God, in me or through me for Your eternal purpose?" This change in perspective brings *life* and opens our hearts to His gentle, training hand.

Read **Romans 8** and focus on verses **26, 28, and 37.**

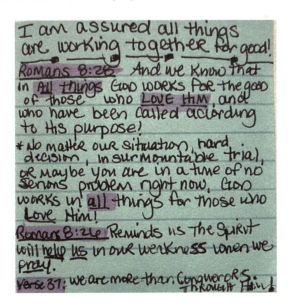

For His Glory | 37

Free from Condemning Charges

The moment you acknowledge you are a sinner, believe on the Lord Jesus Christ, and confess this with your mouth and heart, you are *free*! Free from any past stronghold or bondage. All wrongs are blotted out, and your name is written in the Lamb's book of life. Cleansed. Pure. *Free*.

Now you have a choice each day. Walk in it. Walk in the joy of your freedom through Christ Jesus, and as He allows, tell others about it! Whether you have known the Lord for days or decades, choose to walk in the joy of His freedom today. Regardless of circumstances, our hearts and minds can be free as we choose to rest in His peace.

Thank You, precious Father! Hallelujah!

Deeply Rooted in Him

Some of the live oak trees in my backyard have been there for decades. They are sprawling, some many feet in diameter around the trunk, with canopies that shade the entire house and much of our property. I think of how deeply rooted these trees have to be to hold all the weight and to withstand all the storms, droughts, and freezes, as well as the many birds and animals living within the branches.

How can we be deeply rooted in God? How do we stand in the midst of the spiritual storms, droughts, and freezes in our lives and still provide for others by His love?

It is only possible through our relationship with Him, cultivated by His Word, prayer, and Spirit.

Read context in the Word in **Jeremiah** and in **Psalms** and work through your personal questions.

Pray with me: *Thank You, Father, that we can be deeply rooted in You. Father, stir up a heart's cry to want more and more of You so that our leaves may always be green and our fruit abundant, no matter our circumstances. Amen.*

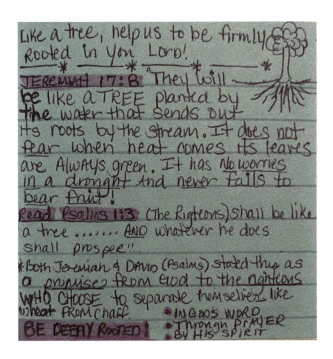

Established, Anointed, and Sealed by God

"Now He who establishes us with you in Christ and has anointed us is God, who also has sealed us and given us the Spirit in our hearts as a guarantee." **(2 Cor. 1:21–22)**

Thank you, Lord, that the moment we chose to give our lives to You, we became Yours—completely and fully Yours. You anointed us, God, set Your seal upon us, and deposited Your Spirit in us the moment we chose to believe.

Let us rejoice and walk each day on the firm foundation of Christ in confidence only of who Christ is in and through us!

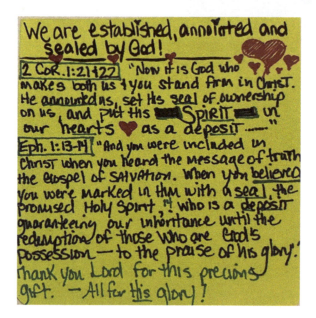

God Will Complete the Good Work He Started in Us

"Being confident of this very thing, that He who has begun a good work in you will complete it until the day of Jesus Christ" **(Phil. 1:6).**

Praise, glory, and thanks to our Father who knows just what we need. He is the Master Potter, He is the most wonderful and gentle teacher, and He knows every plan He has for us.

In the midst of our messy lives, despite our human weakness, His mercy and grace extend to each of us as we turn fully to Him. One by one, He breaks chains, heals wounds, and raises us up to do the good work He created us to do. He is faithful to complete this work until the day He calls us to our eternal home with Him.

He gives us new hearts and instructs and teaches us, by His Spirit, until completion.

> GOD Will Complete the GOOD WORK He Started in Us!
>
> Phil. 1:6 "...being confident of this, that HE who began a GOOD work in You will carry it on to Completion until the day of Christ Jesus."
>
> How? Ezekiel 36:26 "I will give you a new heart ♥ AND put a new SPIRIT within you; and I will remove the heart of stone from your flesh and give you a heart of flesh."
>
> Psalm 32:8 "I will instruct you and teach you in the way which you should go; I will counsel you with My eye upon you."

God Brings Light and Life to the Darkest Places

Let's glorify God today! Praise Him! Just start to thank Him and proclaim who He is. Invite in His presence right where you are. God is there. Go ahead, talk out loud if you need to. He is there.

His presence is *light* and *life*. No matter the darkness that may surround us in this world, in our country, or in a particular circumstance, our God is our *sovereign* Lord! He is always a flame in the dark. His remnant remains, even if we don't always see it with our physical eyes. His Spirit is with us and within us today. His light can never be put out: it *is* eternal.

Glory to God! It doesn't matter where you are. It could be your morning devotional time, or you may be in the car, at the workplace, or at a family member's house, but you can *always* pause to glorify Him and step into His presence of light and life right where you are (just to share a few personal examples).

Let's pray: *Thank you, Lord, for helping us. We are the vessels you use to help bear that light in the world today. May we step into Your light and be* **bold** *and* **bright!**

"For it is the God who commanded light to shine out of darkness, who has shone in our hearts to give the light of the knowledge of the glory of God in the face of Jesus Christ." **(2 Cor. 4:6)**

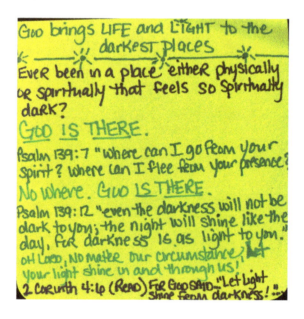

Our Refuge and Strength

When in a tight, difficult, stressful, sorrowful, or extreme circumstance, how do you respond? Think about your character: Do you get angry? Are you anxious? Do you worry or try to take matters into your own hands? Do you attempt to fix it yourself or get depressed or impatient?

First, let me say that we are *human*, and we all struggle with responses like these. Self-reflect and be *honest*. Ask the Lord to search your heart and speak to you about responses you may struggle with the most. When the Lord starts to expose your weakness, confess it and talk to Him about it. Humble yourself and be *honest* with Him. He already knows!

In every circumstance, the Lord wants us to look to Him, to *run* to Him!

Oh, Lord, let our response be to immediately turn to You!

We have to *choose* to take refuge in Him.

Let's pray and talk to Him: *Lord, no matter our circumstance, You are our refuge and our strength. You always see right where we are, and You know our every need. Search my heart, Lord, and help me understand where You want to do a work in my heart so that my response is always to look to You. Help us, Lord, to stand on Your Word, to believe in the faithfulness of Your promises, and to walk by Your strength. Amen.*

Talk to Him, self-reflect, dive into the referenced scriptures, and don't forget to work through your three personal questions.

> God is our refuge and strength!
> Psalm 46:1 God is our refuge and strength, a very present help in trouble.
> Psalm 71:3 Be my strong refuge, to which I may resort continually... ...For You ARE my Rock and my Fortress!
> Psalm 28:7 The LORD is my strength and my shield; My heart trusts Him, and I am helped; Therefore my heart greatly rejoices, and with my song I will praise Him.
> Look to the Lord, believe His word, trust Him and Thank Him. Praise You Lord!

Our Strong Tower

"The name of the Lord is a strong tower; the righteous run to it and are safe" **(Prov. 18:10).**

What a precious promise! We have reflected on areas in our character where the Lord wants us to remember to take refuge in Him. Let's also remember the actions we have to choose to take. We have to *choose to look* to Him, we have *to choose to run* to the tower for us to be safe according to His promise.

A *strong tower* is a reference from ancient times—a fortified, protected tower within the walls of a protected fortress. Go ahead and look up a few different definitions and note the descriptions that stand out to you.

In the presence of our God, we are within His arms—a tower that can never be shaken, penetrated, or destroyed. His loving protection and resting place are eternal. It is who He is.

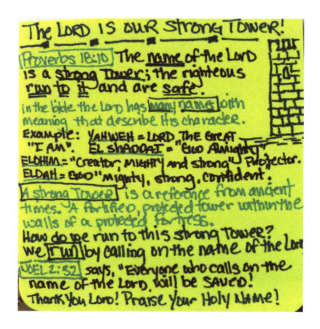

His Love Endures Forever

Those who know me well know that one of my favorite scriptures is **1 Corinthians 13:8,** "Love never fails."

Admittedly, I've been told I have a *lot* of favorite scriptures. Not a bad thing, right? Well, this one I cherish as it is a bold and powerful promise. Love *never* fails. It doesn't just work on Mondays and Wednesdays or when you are at church service or feeling particularly kind. God's love received *never* fails. When *you* choose to walk in *love*, it will *never* fail! How amazing is that?

When we love Him and receive His love, we can then love others with His love. He is the same yesterday, today, and forever.

Do you need a fresh realization of this today? Read through the context of the scripture and talk to Him.

Who can you share this with today? It won't fail, and it always pays dividends, even if we may not see it with our physical eyes at the moment!

Perfect Love Casts Out Fear

Has fear ever stopped you in your tracks?

I can remember a time I was walking through my backyard on a cut path next to tall grass and a fence line. One of my little nieces was with me. Out of the corner of my eye, I saw a snake creeping through the tall grass along the fence. I froze where I was, but my sweet niece was ahead of me and out of arm's reach and she had no idea of the nearby danger. I realized quickly that my next response would directly influence her response: frozen inaction could put her in danger; erratic overreaction could also put her in danger and just scare the poor girl! I quickly and simply prayed, "Lord, help us and keep that snake at bay." At that very moment, I heard His shepherd's voice say, "Walk." He gave us the boldness to quickly and safely walk on the cut path past the snake, who didn't even react to us being there. Afterward, it was a great teachable moment for my niece and me, both in God's help and mercy and the danger of snakes!

In the spiritual life, has Satan, the vilest snake, ever stopped you in your tracks? How much greater is our God through His love in us, perfectly equipping us against the tricks of Satan in every time of need? His perfect love casts out all fear. He equips us by His Spirit and will set a safe and clear path before us. Think about how your response in the moment impacts others for Him.

Will you *believe* in who He is, ask for His help, and boldly step forward in His clear path by His Spirit and love?

> **Perfect Love casts out Fear**
> 1 John 4:16-19 "And we have known and believed the love that God has for us. God is love, and he who abides in love abides in God, and God in him." Love has been perfected among us in this: that we may have boldness in the day of Judgement; because as He is, so are we in this world. ¹⁸There is no fear in love; but perfect love casts out fear, because fear involves torment. But he who fears has not been made perfect in love." We love Him because He first loved us.
> Will you BELIEVE in who He is, ask for His help, and boldly step forward in His clear path by the Spirit in His love?

The Bread of Life

Ever been hungry or thirsty to the point where it hurts or you can't sleep? Maybe even a bit "hangry?" (I just couldn't resist.)

In **John 6**, Jesus declares that He is the bread of life. All who come to Him will never go hungry, and all who believe will never thirst. Well, we know that He can provide for all of our physical needs. However, this promise is so much deeper. This is for every spiritual need. He can meet it all: every desire, hunger, and thirst of our hearts and souls. This is life for us on this earth and leads us to eternal life with Him in acceptance of and belief in Him as our Lord and Savior.

Are you spiritually hungry? Thirsty? Pull up a chair to His table and commune with Him today. He's always waiting for you.

Let's pray: *Thank you, Lord, that as we look to You and believe, You meet our every need, our every "hunger" and "thirst." Help us press into You and walk fully satisfied in You within us. Deepen our relationship with You, Jesus. Amen.*

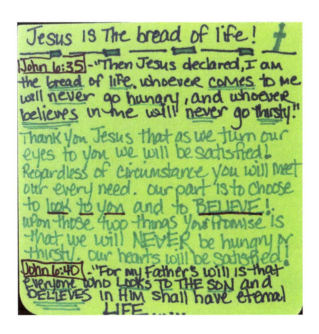

Living Water

In the days when Jesus walked the earth, there were times He traveled in areas that had very little fresh water. Most of us are so used to our modern-day privilege of turning a faucet on and getting all the fresh water needed. We can even purchase it bottled in every variety we can think of: still, carbonated, flavored, distilled. In His Word, "living water" refers to *moving or flowing* water—rivers, streams, etc.—water that is not still or stagnant. Since His region had few rivers or streams, wells were the primary source of fresh water.

"Whoever believes in me, as Scripture has said, rivers of living water will flow from within them" **(John 7:38 NIV).**

It is by design that Jesus referred to Himself as "living water." He described Himself this way to the Samaritan woman He met at Jacob's well. What a picture! By His Spirit living within us, He brings life and full satisfaction of thirst with living water that is fresh, pure, and life-giving.

It can flow from within us to be poured out to others for His glorious purpose. Jump into His river today.

Dive into the context of the scripture referenced.

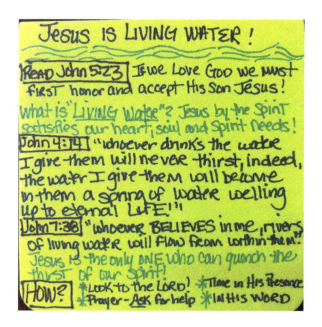

The Gate

Read the context of **John 10**; focus on verses 7–9.

> Then Jesus said to them again, "Most assuredly I say to you, I am the door of the sheep. All who ever came before Me are thieves and robbers, but the sheep did not hear them. I am the door. If anyone enters by Me, he will be saved, and will go in and out and find pasture. **(John 10:7–9 NKJV)**

In Old Testament times, the "sheep's gate" or "door" was designed in Jerusalem for animals to be brought in from the countryside for sacrifice or atonement of sins. It was a one-way door, friends; the sheep never came back out!

Jesus is saying He is the *new door*—the *way*. He became the sacrifice for our sin through the work on the cross. Why? Abundant life for us! We have a way out of our sinful lives and the opportunity to live our lives for Him.

Pray with me: *Thank you, Lord, for the work You did for us on the cross! Your sacrifice and new covenant with us give us the precious gift of abundant, eternal life! Thank you, Lord, that you are the* way, *the* door, *the* new gate! *Through You, Lord, we find our salvation, life, and rest.*

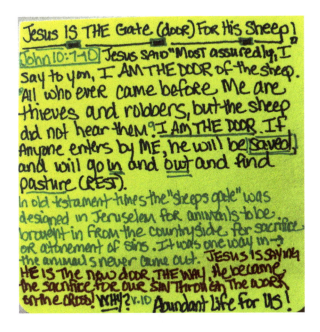

The Lord Hears Our Heart's Cry

"The eyes of the Lord are on the righteous, / And His ears are open to their cry" **(Ps. 34:15).**

    The Lord hears the cry of our hearts—His righteous ones. Why is the righteous part important? We are to have right and pure hearts before Him. Let me be clear: I'm not saying we have to be perfect for Him to hear us. We will *never* be perfect; it is why we *need* Jesus! I'm a mess in the flesh living by His grace each day!

    We have pure hearts before Him by humbling ourselves and asking for forgiveness for sin with pure motives; then, we are free. He hears us in our sinful flesh cry out for forgiveness as He molds and shapes our character over time. It's in this place of purity of heart and motive that we commune with our Father, and He hears us! When we talk to Him, He always knows the motives of our hearts. While He's working on our character and making us more like Him, He hears our cry for all things: trials, family needs, desires of our hearts, requests for direction—everything.

    He pours out His love and mercy for us in this place, into any heart ready to receive it.

"Neither do people pour new wine into old wineskins. If they do, the skins will burst: the wine will run out and the wineskins will be ruined. No, they pour new wine into new wineskins and both are preserved" **(Matt. 9:17 NIV)**

Dive into each scripture and talk to Him about your three personal questions.

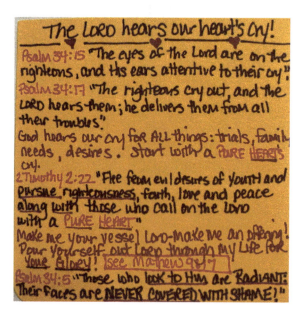

Stand Still in His Peace

Have you ever been in that place where you are crying out to the Lord over a circumstance and waiting on a word, an answer, or a breakthrough? Ever feel like you are having to do it day after day after day?

He knows.

Every time I've been in that place, God has used it for my good to teach me something, to speak a powerful word in time, or to help me grow as I seek Him in the waiting.

Yes, waiting.

If you are seeking Him and still unsure of His answer or do not yet see the outcome, then you are called to *wait*. Wait on Him; *rest* in Him.

This is hard for us humans, especially those of us who are ready to "fix it" or come up with creative ways to solve things or think we just know how.

Trust me, God doesn't need our help!

"The Lord will fight for you; you need only to be still" **(Exod. 14:14 NIV).**

I love this scripture as it is both a *promise* and *direction*.
Explore the context of the scripture provided below and talk to Him.

Let's pray in the words of the psalmist: *Thank you, Lord, for being "our refuge, strength, / A very present help in time of trouble" (Ps. 46:1). You are the mighty true King who understands our weaknesses and patiently teaches us in our waiting and resting in You. Thank you, Lord, for being our strength and shield. In Your name, Jesus, I pray and trust as I wait. Amen.*

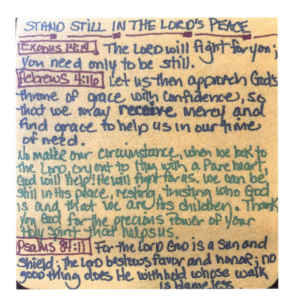

Our Defender

Read **Psalm 31.**

    This is a beautiful prayer and heart cry to the Lord. Even in the midst of severe, life-threatening circumstances, the psalmist, David, pours it all out at our Lord's feet. He takes refuge in Him. He is thankful. He proclaims who God is and resolves to put all trust in God. He rejoices! He puts *his whole life* in His hands. This is all in the midst of David's circumstances, before God delivers him.

    What an example for us. The Lord sees our hearts in this. How much of our lives do we choose to trust Him with? How often? Can we thank Him, praise Him, and rejoice in Him in the midst? He is always faithful to meet us by His Spirit.

    It is time to self-reflect, and there is no time to waste.

    Our God is our *defender* and mighty *fortress* in *all* areas of life if we *let* Him.

    What a promise we have as we take courage in Him; He strengthens our hearts as we hope in Him **(**See **Ps. 31:24).**

> **God is our Defender!**
> Read Psalms chapter 31 This is a beautiful example of a pure heart's cry to the Lord, trusting, rejoicing and resting in His abundant Mercy! How?
> V.1 Take refuge in Him!
> V.2 Cry out to Him w/ a pure heart.
> V.7 Be thankful, glad in whom the Lord is. REJOICE!
> V.8 He will set your feet in a spacious or wide open place. Meaning freedom, peace for your heart and mind.
> V.14 Regardless of visible circumstance Put your Trust in the Lord and Who HE IS.
> V.15 Truly put your life in His hands — Let
> V.23 LOVE THE LORD faithful believers Go!
> He preserves those true to Him!
> V.24 BE STRONG, TAKE HEART All you who hope in the Lord! STAND ON HIS Promises!

Nothing Can Suppress the Power of God

I'll never forget this word from God.

Have you ever been at the end of every ounce of strength within you? I remember a Saturday morning when my sweet husband was on shift, and I was up early attempting to commune with our Lord before our regular Saturday morning food pantry serve at church. I was asking the Lord to give a word for our volunteers that day as we dedicated the start of the day to Him. I knew there would be so many families in need, so many hardships to pray for. Food is just one physical need the Lord uses us to meet. More importantly, we share the love of God and the truth of Christ, and we have a prayer ministry right at car side.

The challenge this particular morning was that I was empty, exhausted, discouraged, and overwhelmed. Stressed from long hours at my workplace, I was overwhelmed by the needs of so many people and physically exhausted from minimal rest. In addition to all of this, my heart had been hurt by someone close. In tears, I had to fight to give over the hurt so that I could love and not give way to offense in my heart.

In a brief moment, I fell facedown to the floor of my living room on the carpet just *crying out* to our God. The tears slowly gave way to words of praise, and our faithful Father lifted my head and my heart for the day's work ahead.

He did more. He did miracles through prayer that day for many. Our Father woke up a sweet friend of mine and told her to come to our church that day. She didn't know it was the pantry serve, but she came to the church. This precious woman will *run* to you to grab what you are carrying and lighten your load; she serves with all of her heart in so many ways. However, on this day, she just sat in a chair in the sanctuary. After noticing her, I kept asking the Lord, "Lord, where would You have me ask her to help?" No answer.

Finally, she waved me over and said, "Sister Darlene, I have been sitting here and watching. The Lord told me to come today, and I didn't even know there was a pantry serve. But the Lord has given me a word that I must tell you."

Okay, I thought.

She proceeded to say, "*Nothing* can suppress the power of God."

It hit my heart, and my knees hit the floor. I immediately knew my Father was saying that He is King. He is sovereign. He is omnipotent and omniscient. There is *nothing—no thing,* no physical entity or circumstance—that can suppress His power! It doesn't matter how I feel or the challenge I may be facing. His grace is sufficient, and when we ask for His strength, His power will move through us. In His love for me, He even woke up a faithful sister in Christ and sent His word through her! Thank you, Lord!

Dive into His scripture referenced below and talk to Him about your personal questions.

> NOTHING can suppress the Power of GOD!
> Psalm 113 v.1 Praise His name!
> v.5 There is No one Like Him!
> GOD is sovereign, Mighty, omnipotent, omnipresent, omniscient! Lord of Lord! King of Kings!
> Jeremiah 10:12 IT IS HE who made the earth by His POWER, who established the world by his wisdom –
> Psalm 66:7 who rules by His Might FOREVER whose eyes keep watch on the nations –
> How do we apply God's Power to our own lives?
> BELIEVE! The only thing that can dampen the power of GOD in your own life is unbelief!
> John 11:40 Did I not tell you that if you believe you will see the Glory of GOD!"
> Matthew 19:26 with man this is impossible, with GOD All Things ARE Possible!
> Zech 4:6 Not by (our) might or power, but by THE SPIRIT!

Prince of Peace

"Let the peace of God rule in your hearts, to which indeed you were called in one body. And be thankful" **(Col. 3:15 ESV)**.

Anyone or anything promising peace is not authentic or true without Christ. No self-help book, no secluded place in another part of the world, no one person can give us lasting peace. Christ is the source. We have to believe it and receive it. Because of Christ, we have peace with God our Father and can commune with Him. *Peace* is a fruit of the Spirit! When we choose to rest in Him, we can walk in His gift of peace.

Thank Him. Thank Him in all circumstances as you pray, and He will guard your heart and mind. Rest in His peace as you walk with Him each day.

> Jesus is the Prince of Peace!
> Col. 3:15 Let the Peace of God Rule your heart and be thankful!
> What does it mean to let Peace rule in our heart? Anything or Anyone promising peace is not being Authentic. TRUE & Lasting soul-level peace is only found in Jesus Christ. The Source of All Peace!
> 2 Thess. 3:16 Now may the Lord of peace himself give you peace at All times in every way!
> Romans 5:1 Since we have been Justified through faith we have Peace with God THROUGH our Lord JESUS CHRIST!
> Phil 4:6-7 Do not be Anxious! In every situation by prayer and petition with Thanksgiving present your requests to God. And the PEACE of God will guard your HEART and MIND IN CHRIST JESUS!

The Good Shepherd

Jesus is our Good Shepherd. Have you ever put much thought into what a shepherd really does? Not too many of us have even been close to a flock of sheep, much less know what it takes to watch over them.

A shepherd tends to, herds, and leads sheep to pasture that is safe, leads them to water, watches over them by night, and protects them from predators and all kinds of sickness. It is a twenty-four seven job.

Jesus is our Good Shepherd who lays down His life for His sheep. We are like little sheep who can't eat, sleep, or be safe without our shepherd. He constantly watches over us, guards us, guides us, and cares for our every need!

It may seem like a simple concept; however, I know sometimes I need a fresh revelation of my absolute need for Him. Take time to reflect on your personal relationship with our Shepherd and the scripture provided.

> Jesus is the Good Shepherd!
>
> John 10:11 "I am the good shepherd. The good shepherd lays down his life for the sheep."
>
> A shepherd: A person who tends, herds, feeds or guards herds of sheep.
>
> John 10:14 "I am the good shepherd. I know my sheep and my sheep know me, just as the Father knows me and I know the Father - and I lay down my life for the sheep."
>
> Jesus Christ is the ULTIMATE shepherd! The one who watches over us, guards us, guides us, and cares for our every need!
>
> Lord, help us to listen to your voice and follow you!

The First Noel

Only the Lord knows the time of year you are reading this, but shouldn't we celebrate the good news of our Savior all year?

Jesus and His birth are the true reasons we sing the song "The First Noel."

Across languages, there may be different ways to say the phrase, but all point to the meaning of the root word, *Noel*. For example, *Joyeux Noel* (French) means "Merry Christmas." The French word *nouvelles* means "news." A Middle English word *nowel* means "A shout of joy" or "Christmas song." The French word *Noel* comes from the Latin *natalis* meaning birthday.

The Word of God explains it for us in **Luke 2**. Read this chapter. The angels shouted and proclaimed the coming of Jesus and glorified God.

Let us also shout for *joy* and proclaim the good news of our Savior's birth! The most perfect gift of Jesus and the salvation available for eternal life with Him in heaven are meant to be shared! We are called to this all year long, Amen?

"How beautiful are the feet of those who preach the gospel of peace, Who bring glad tidings of good things!" **(Rom. 10:15 NKJV).**

Rejoice! Unto Us, a Savior Is Born

"Rejoice in the Lord always. Again, I say rejoice!" **(Phil. 4:4)**.

Do you know this in your heart, but have a hard time *doing* it? Just start to thank Him. This simple act is actually one of trust and love. As you thank Him, it becomes easier to praise Him and His Spirit of joy.

Our God is mighty, sovereign, gentle, and merciful! What a precious gift He has given us in Jesus. We have the opportunity to be *eternally free* and covered by His sacrifice on the cross!

I find that I have to make a choice to walk in this joy! I have to be reminded, at times, of the joy and blessing of all He has done for me.

This simple and powerful message is for us to walk in daily. His son, Jesus, is so wonderful. How easy it can become for us to take this for granted.

Let's pray: Lord, I choose Your joy today. I ask for help as I thank You. Thank You for giving us Your Son Jesus. Thank You for the work He did on the cross. Thank You for the gift of salvation and freedom, Lord. Thank You for the example Christ is for us in how we should walk daily. Help me, Lord, to walk in Your joy and to be ready to testify of who You are as You lead me. Glory to You, God!

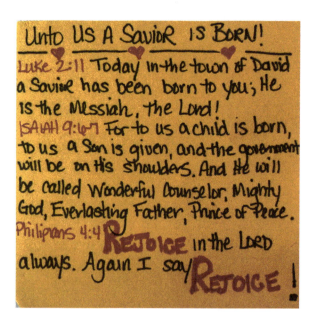

El Roi: The God Who Sees Me

The Lord sees you. He sees *you.*

Read **Genesis 16:6–14**. This is the story of Hagar. Mistreated by Sarai, Abram's wife, she fled into the desert alone, pregnant and hurt in her heart.

I love that the Word says in verse 7, "An angel of the Lord found her." God met her right where she was and satisfied every need. On that day, Hagar gave God an additional name in Hebrew: *El Roi,* meaning "You are the God who sees me."

I love this so much! She didn't just say, you are the God who sees (although He does see all things!). She proclaimed, "You are the God who sees *me!*"

No matter your circumstances, God sees *you.* You are so precious to the Lord. He is the one who created you and is in control of all things. Will you resolve in your heart to trust Him, believe His promises, and thank Him for all things? Look to Him.

Resolve in your heart to make your plans *His* plans. God sees you and knows your every need. Let Him help you today.

The Great "I AM"

"And God said to Moses, 'I AM WHO I AM.' And He said, 'Thus you shall say to the children of Israel, 'I AM has sent me to you''" **(Exod. 3:14).**

Think about this: I AM—two small words and just three letters! So simple, yet so *powerful* a statement and the most profound name we can believe in. Two small words say it all about our most awesome God. He just *is*! He is our everything.

There is no limit to how we can unceasingly call and rely upon Him. He is forever and eternal in all His ways.

Pray about and proclaim who He is for you. Don't forget to talk to Him about your three personal questions!

Let us pray: *Father, You are both our sovereign, holy King and our tender, loving Father. God, You are the Master of Miracles, the supernatural Creator of everything, the one who fulfills our every need. You validate us. You give us hope and a future, God. You are our infallible guide on our path in life. You are the great "I AM!"*

Seek First His Kingdom

Have you ever asked any of the following questions:

How do I live a life in Christ?

How do I walk a life according to His will?

How do I have faith when I seem to struggle with _____ (you fill in the blank)?"

We have the most wonderful promises.

"Because of the Lord's great love, we are not consumed, for His compassions never fail. They are new every morning; great is Your faithfulness. I say to myself, 'The Lord is my portion; therefore, I will wait for Him'" **(Lam. 3:22–24 NIV)**.

"But his delight is in the law of the Lord, / And His law he meditates day and night. / He shall be like a tree / Planted by the rivers of water, / That brings forth its fruit in its season, / Whose leaf also shall not wither; / And whatever he does shall prosper" **(Ps. 1:2–3 NKJV)**.

His instructions are simple in **Matthew 6:33**: Seek *first* the Kingdom of God. Seek Him *first*.

Read **Matthew 6** in context and talk to Him about what it means to you to seek Him first. As we do this, all things fall in order, even if we don't yet see how. This is living a life in Him.

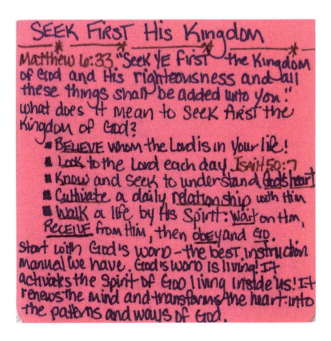

For His Glory | 61

Fellowship with the Lord

What does *fellowship* mean? Go ahead, look it up. You will find definitions like "friendly association." Associated words are *companionship*, *comradeship*, etc. I personally also think of the word *commune*. I want to fellowship and commune with the Lord.

We can have fellowship with our heavenly Father and commune with Him as a friend.

"You are My friends if you do whatever I command you. No longer do I call you servants, for a servant does not know what his master is doing; but I have called you friends, for all things that I heard from My Father I have made known to you" **(John 15:14–15)**.

Read **1 John 1:1–4**. The disciples shared how by being one in His spirit, we can have fellowship with God and His Son. By sharing with others, we can also have fellowship with one another.

It's only by abiding in Him and receiving His love that we can have fellowship with and love others.

Let us pray: *Lord, my heart desires to know You more, to walk with You each day in fellowship, and abide in You. Thank You for continuing to teach us each day as we are willing to receive, building our ever-increasing faith. Thank you, Lord.*

God Is Light

God is light and in Him is no darkness at all. If we say that we have fellowship with Him, and walk in darkness, we lie and do not practice truth. But if we walk in the light as He is in the light, we have fellowship with one another and the blood of Jesus Christ His Son cleanses us from all sin, **(1 John 1:5–7)**

In contrasting light and darkness, the Lord simplifies for us the power of who He is for us. Through the work He did on the cross, through our repentant hearts, and by our acceptance of Him, He *transforms* our hearts and minds over time as He draws us into His truthful light. It's in this place, His presence, in fellowship and communion, that we can have a relationship with Him, which allows us to love others with His love.

One small candle with a flame can illuminate one large room, being seen from every dark corner and every angle. It pierces and overtakes the darkness. Thank you, Lord, for drawing us to You, into Your light, *setting us apart* within the darkness of a sinful world, and setting us on a lampstand for Your glory!

Read **1 John 1–2**. Don't forget to talk to our Father about your three personal questions.

Let's pray: *Lord, thank You for Your Son, Jesus, the light of the world and, through His sacrifice, the perfect atonement for our sin. Thank You for Your Word and for helping us understand Your heart for us.*

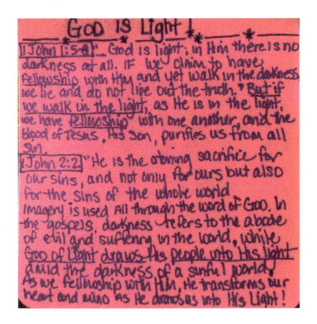

Set Apart

Read **2 Timothy 2:19–22** and the rest of the chapter for context. Verse 21 says, "Therefore, if anyone cleanses himself from what is dishonorable, he will be a vessel for honorable use, set apart as holy, useful to the master of the house, ready for every good work."

This example, in context, refers to a "great" house which was a house of elite residents within a city that contained vessels of gold, silver, wood, and clay. In that time, gold and silver may be reserved for elite residents, while common people or servants used wood or clay. The Lord says that *when we cleanse ourselves*, meaning to repent before Him with a pure heart, we *become* vessels of honorable use—honorable vessels set apart for God's good work!

"Create in me a clean heart, O God, / and renew a right spirit within me" **(Ps. 51:10 ESV).**

Our Father sees us right where we are. He sees our hearts, every intent, and every motive. By His Spirit, He changes us, and by His blood shed on the cross, we can be purified, sanctified, and redeemed.

Will you ask Him with me today?

Let's pray: *Lord, help us to live lives completely set apart for Your glory! Oh Lord, raise up a desire in our hearts to let You examine us. Examine my heart, Lord, and purify me for Your good work.*

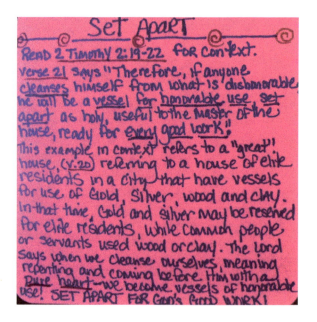

Be Still and Wait

Psalm 46:10 NKJV says, "Be still, and know that I am God; / I will be exalted among the nations, / I will be exalted in the earth!"

We live in a rushed, crazed, chaotic world that at times can seem overwhelming or defeating. Our God knows and sees. He is in control of it all, even when it seems out of control.

He is a refuge for us, an ever-present help in times of trouble (*See* **Ps. 46:1**).

Read **Psalms 46** and **27**. Our God is *sovereign* and in control of all things! *All*.

Call on the Lord. Believe in Him, wait on Him, be of good courage, and He will strengthen you (*See* **Ps. 27:13–14**).

The Lord is so faithful, and His mercy endures forever. Amid our busy lives and in every circumstance, He wants us to remember to look to Him first, call on Him *first*, *be still* in the most turbulent times, and *wait* on His word. He is merciful, in control, has all authority, and He sees *you*. Remain confident only in Him. Be still, be strong, and wait on the Lord!

Living in Love for Others

This week, I was reminded of the greatest gift of love: our precious Savior, Jesus. I'm thankful for the Holy Spirit given to us freely, and that, as we ask for help, by His Spirit, we can live and move according to His plan. Living in the love of Christ enables us to live our lives in love for others. Help us, Lord, to live our lives in love for others, and all for Your glory, Lord! As Your Word says, *love never fails*!

"And above all things have fervent love for one another, for 'love will cover a multitude of sins'" **(1 Peter 4:8).**

Read the scriptures below and talk to the Lord about them. Talk to our Lord about how He wants you to love others right where He has placed you. Ask Him how He would have you show His love today and each day.

> **LIVING IN LOVE FOR OTHERS**
>
> 1 Peter 4:8-10 "Above all love each other deeply, because love covers a multitude of sins. Each of you should use whatever gift you have recieved to serve others, as faithful stewards of God's grace in its various forms."
>
> Galatians 5:13-14 "You, my brothers and sisters, were called to be free. But do not use your freedom to indulge the flesh; rather, serve one another humbly in love. For the entire law is fulfilled in keeping this one command: "Love your neighbor as yourself".
>
> As believers in Christ full of His Spirit, the Lord changes us and molds us producing Christlike character in us. We are set apart, and the greatest gift of the Lord we can exhibit is LOVE. We are called to serve one another in LOVE!

Present Your Requests before God

Read **Philippians 4:6–7 NIV** and the context in which it was written: "Do not be anxious about anything, but in every situation, by prayer and petition, with thanksgiving present your requests to God. And the peace of God which transcends all understanding, will guard your hearts and minds in Christ Jesus."

This is one of my favorite verses because it gives us direction for each day tied with a wonderful promise.

Our instruction: Don't be anxious. Be thankful and talk to our heavenly Father about everything.

Our promise: Peace and He will guard our hearts and minds.

It is easy to read this scripture, but admittedly, the instruction is not always easy to do. Do you ever struggle with being anxious or worrying? Is your natural reaction to pray? If you do pray, do you struggle with focusing in your prayer time, or do you battle with other thoughts that interrupt? I'm asking these questions because I have experienced each of these in my personal walk. I have learned to fight my battles according to the Lord's way and by His Spirit and to take action in obedience to His Word. This allows me to walk freely in His promise.

How? I'll share my personal testament:

- I *look to God* and confess how I'm feeling. If I'm feeling anxious or worried, I *choose* to take those thoughts captive **(See 2 Cor. 10:5)**.
- I don't allow my thoughts to dwell on the worries or emotions of my circumstance. If my thoughts are worrisome or open the doors for lies from the enemy that hurt my heart, I resist the enemy and call him out **(See James 4:7)**.
- I start to *thank* the Lord. I speak out loud to Him and declare how wonderful He is. I sing to Him praises and thanksgiving. This drowns out the anxiousness and allows me to pray.
- I then unashamedly lay all my thoughts before Him. So many times, this happens while I'm driving or on a long walk. I just tell Him all. Sometimes, speaking out loud to Him or writing it down helps me to focus.

This next part is important:

- I *surrender*: I surrender the situation and requests; I surrender my own ideas of what His answer should look like; I surrender and lay it at His feet.

Have I had to do this more than once for the same situation at times? Yes. However, I can share that each time I have, it becomes easier and easier to do. In *every circumstance*, this leads to His peace in my heart and mind *every* time.

Reference each scripture and talk to Him about your three personal questions. Is there a request you should surrender at His feet today?

> **In every situation, Present Your Requests Before God**
> — * — * — * —
> Philippians 4:6-7 "Do not be anxious about anything, but in every situation, by prayer and petition, with thanksgiving, present your requests to God. And the PEACE OF GOD which transcends all understanding, will Guard your hearts and minds in Christ Jesus."
> What a wonderful Promise! Doing this may not always be easy! God wants us to continually look to Him no matter the circumstance. In good times, and in the most heart-wrenching difficulties He says in Every situation to Praise + Thank Him. In His mercy, He stands for us, Fights for us, Lifts us and Guards us!

Pressing Onward

"But one thing I do: Forgetting what is behind and straining forward to what is ahead, I press on toward the goal to win the prize for which God has called me heavenward in Christ Jesus" **(Phil. 3:13–14 NIV).**

This example that God gives us in Paul is so amazing. Paul was a vessel of God who had a heart's desire to live fully for the Lord. However, we know that wasn't always the case before he knew Christ! God amazingly changed his life. Paul went from a man who used to murder Christians to a man God used to spread the gospel to other countries—to the "ends of the earth." Paul was a man who became the Lord's, but, he was also rejected, hunted, beaten, imprisoned, and starved all for the sake of Christ's name. He was also *delivered* from every situation, and God performed many miracles through him and on his behalf.

God's love, power, and provision are no different for us today.

Let's pray: Oh Lord, no matter the circumstance, I choose to press on toward the upward call of Jesus Christ, for Your glory, Lord, and knowing I'll be with You eternally in heaven one day.

Pressing Onward

Phil 3:13-14 "... But one thing I do. Forgetting what is behind and straining forward to what is ahead, I press on toward the goal to win the prize for which God has called me heavenward in Christ Jesus."

Think about Paul's example, how God amazingly molded and changed his life. A man who use to murder Christians to a man God used to spread the Gospel to other countries and to the "ends" of the earth. God delivered Paul from every horrible circumstance. When Paul said "I press onward" it means he chose to move forward to the most amazing prize. Our promised gift of eternal life with Him in heaven!

Christlike Humility

"Fulfill my joy by being like-minded, having the same love, being of one accord, of one mind. Let nothing be done through selfish ambition or conceit, but in lowliness of mind let each esteem others better than himself" **(Phil. 2:2–4 NKJV).**

Let's think about this word *humble*. Words that come to mind to describe it are not proud, not haughty, and unpretentious. One definition refers to being humble in spirit or manner. Go ahead and look up a few different definitions of the word *humble*. My favorite is the word *servant*: having a servant's heart and mind.

Read **Philippians 2:1–8** in context. We are instructed to have a mindset like Christ. Christ was born on this earth in the humblest of circumstances—a small baby in a manger. He walked this earth with the heart and nature of a servant. He humbled Himself unto His Father God, even unto death on the cross.

Let's pray: *Lord, give us a new and fresh revelation of what it means to* humble *ourselves before You. To walk in this life with a* servant's *heart and mind in love for You and others. Help us to live in love for others and all for Your glory each day!*

How might you humble yourself today? Don't forget to talk to our Father about your three personal questions and let Him work in your heart.

Offense Separates, but Love Conquers

The devil has no new tricks, and he gets no glory. However, it is important that we are wise in the Lord and recognize his tricks by the Spirit of the Lord. Satan will do anything he can to tear down the body of Christ and bring division.

Read **Galatians 5:19–21,** which lists the fruit or works of the flesh. Two that I see the enemy commonly try to use to divide God's people are *contentions* and *dissensions*. The Oxford dictionary defines them in this way:

Contention—anger between two people who disagree.

Dissensions—disagreement, difference of opinion, conflict, friction, strife, argument, or quarreling.

Contentions and dissensions can come from or lead to offense in the heart.

Offense—the feeling of being upset or angry at something that somebody has said or done.

"He who covers a transgression seeks love, but he who repeats a matter separates friends" **(Prov. 17:9).**

Offense in the heart separates friends and family. I think of the picture of how offense puts a fence between friends.

God has already conquered Satan and has made a way for us to walk freely and put the enemy under our feet: *love.*

Reference and read **Galatians 5:14–16.** I encourage you to read all of Galatians 5. Walking by the Spirit produces the fruit of the Spirit and extinguishes *all* attempts of the enemy **(See Gal. 5:22–23).**

Talk to the Lord about your three personal questions. Take the time to empty your heart before Him and let go of anything that may be causing contention, dissension, or offense in your heart. We can't do this on our own; it is a work of the Holy Spirit. Ask Him to help you forgive. Ask Him to purify your heart, and walk *freely* in Him to love with His *love.*

Love

Love is a powerful gift. It conquers fears, always perseveres, and endures over time. God loves us so much He gave us His Son, Jesus, so that we may have the promise of salvation and eternal life **(John 3:16)**. Jesus loves us so much He *willingly* died for us on the cross! Love is the greatest gift we can walk in each day.

"And now these three things remain: Faith, Hope, and Love, but the greatest of these is Love" **(1 Cor. 13:13 NIV)**.

When I think about the magnitude of what love *really* is, it is overwhelming to my heart and spirit at times. In a world that continuously tries to redefine what love is, what it should be, and what it should look like, I think it is so important for us to focus on the true meaning of love.

We are called to love the Lord our God with all our hearts, all our minds, and all our souls. The Word says this is the "first and greatest commandment," the second being "Love your neighbor as yourself" (*See* **Matt. 22:27–40**).

You see, we have to *choose to love* God; we have to *choose to receive* His love, and *only* then are we enabled to love others with His love. There is no other way.

Love is the most powerful gift; it is our greatest gift. It never fails.

If we want to walk a Christ-centered life full of His *life* and by His Spirit, we have to understand the magnitude of this gift. Over the next several devotional notes, we will break down and focus on several descriptors of what love is and how we can walk in it.

Read through the scriptures provided. I pray for fresh revelation for your heart as you commune with our Father. Ask our Lord where and how you have opportunities to love Him and to love others with His love.

> **LOVE**
>
> 1 Cor. 13:13 "And now these three things remain: Faith, Hope and Love, but the greatest of these is LOVE."
>
> Description: Love is not based on emotions or feelings. It is a decision to be committed to the well being of others without condition or circumstances.
>
> 1 John 4:7 "Dear friends, let us love one another, for love comes from God. Everyone who loves has been born of God and knows God."
>
> 1 Peter 4:8 "Above All Love each other deeply, because love covers a multitude of sins."
>
> 1 Cor 13:8 "Love Never fails."

Love Is Patient

The last devotional note references the gift of love as a powerful gift—the greatest gift. It is the most excellent way to walk through life.

Read **1 Corinthians 13:1–10.** Highlight or underline all the descriptors of love.

I know this scripture is popular. You see it at weddings and on posters or home décor of all kinds. It's easy to breeze through it. Let's take the time to ask the Lord to help us understand it.

1 Corinthians 13:4 describes love as "patient." Some versions may say "suffers long."

Would you describe yourself typically as a patient person? I have to admit, I'm generally patient, but there are definitely times when my patience is tested!

Being patient in the Lord's love means we are willing to *wait* for God's perfect provision and timing in all circumstances. It means we have to have restraint and impulse control over our responses. This is both in responses that others may see in us and responses within our hearts.

Let's pray: *Lord, help us to be patient as we wait on You each day in Your presence for direction in every circumstance. Help us to be patient with ourselves as we learn to wait on You. Help us to show Your love by being patient with others, both the saved and the lost. Open doors to show Your love and to build up others through our lives, Lord. Help us, Lord, to live our lives loving others because we love You. Amen.*

Read the additional scriptures in context and talk to Him about your three personal questions.

Love Is Kind

First Corinthians 13 continues to describe love as kind. What is kindness? It's considering others to understand what they prefer or need; to be caring.

I love **Proverbs 25:15 NIV:** "Through patience, a ruler can be persuaded, and a gentle tongue can break a bone."

Kindness in speech and love is powerful and can accomplish what may outwardly seem impossible.
Oh, Lord, help us to remember this when someone else slights us, and kindness is not our natural response!
Our Father's kindness and goodness are new for us each day, never ending and unfailing. He can help us, by His Spirit, to love others through kindness.

"Do you despise the riches of His goodness, forbearance, and longsuffering, not knowing that the goodness of God leads you to repentance?" **(Rom. 2:4 NKJV).**

Let us pray: *Father, help us by Your Spirit to be an example of Your kindness, so that others may be drawn to You for the sake of salvation. Amen.*

Love Does Not Envy

Love does not envy. This may seem very elementary, something that we teach small children. However, don't adults struggle with this at times too? Can't we sometimes be like children in the Spirit, needing to mature spiritually to show love in all things including being content, not grumbling, being thankful for blessings, and happy for others' good?

Okay, don't close the book if that hits your heart. Maturity in the Spirit comes by trusting the Lord *in every* circumstance. Put your petitions before Him with a thankful heart, waiting on Him and trusting Him with the outcome. He is always for our good, and His ways are higher than our ways.

We have to choose to look to the Lord in all things, compare our circumstances, and align them with His Word. When we do this, rather than comparing to others or the lives of others, we can see clearly and put the temptation of envy to rest.

Think about how everyone's life (or the false picture created of their life) is online for most to see. How easy is it to evaluate the lives of others with just a few minutes of scrolling through social media?

Let's choose to have a heart of contentment in Him. Read the scriptures and research the context to talk to our Lord about it.

Love Does Not Boast

To further understand how to describe Christ's true love, let's think about the next description in **1 Corinthians 13**.

Our Lord God is sovereign over *all* things, and He gets the glory for all things!

"But God forbid that I should glory, save in the cross of our Lord Jesus Christ, by whom the world was crucified unto me, and I unto the world" **(Gal. 6:14 KJV)**.

Love does not boast, and it is not proud. Be humble; give glory to the Lord and credit to others. Be modest.

Let's pray: *Oh Lord, help us to boast in You, to love others by encouraging them and loving them above ourselves, and to further understand what it means to love others and to live a life all for Your glory!*

Father, in all our imperfections, Your grace is sufficient for us, and Your power is made perfect in weakness. Father, if I boast, I boast in my weaknesses, so that Christ's power may rest on me **(2 Corinthians 12:8–9** author's paraphrase**).**

Read the context of each scripture provided and talk to our heavenly Father.

> Love does not boast, is not Proud
> — ♥ — ♥ — ♥ — ♥ — ♥ — ♥♥ —
> Be humble, give glory to the Lord and credit to others. Be modest. Love others.
> Psalm 34:2 "I will glory in the Lord! Let the afflicted hear and rejoice!"
> Philippians 3:3 "For it is we who are the circumcision, who serve God by His Spirit, who boast in Christ Jesus, and who put no confidence in the flesh."
> Philippians 2:1-4 "Therefore, if you have any encouragement from being united with Christ, if any comfort from His love, if any common sharing in the Spirit, any tenderness and compassion, then make my joy complete by being like-minded, having the same love, being one in spirit and mind. Do nothing out of selfish ambition or vain conceit. In humility value others above yourself, not looking to your interests, but to those of others!"

Love Is Not Rude or Self-Seeking

I love that **1 Corinthians 13** has so many descriptors about love. Thank you, Lord, for helping us understand what it is *not* for the greater goal of understanding what it *is*.

We have to be willing to ask our heavenly Father to help us walk in this each day. No matter our circumstances or how we feel, we need His help in responding in kindness and preferring others above ourselves.

We continue to thank our Lord Jesus for His most precious act of love on the cross that gave us eternal life. He prefers us all over Himself, in love.

Help us, Lord, to be good stewards of the little things and the individuals placed in our lives right at home, for Your greater glory!

"And above all things have fervent love for one another, for 'love will cover a multitude of sins.' Be hospitable to one another without grumbling. As each one has received a gift, minister it to one another, as good stewards of the manifold grace of God" **(1 Peter 4:8–10 NKJV)**.

Read the context of each scripture below and talk to Him about your three personal questions. Let Him do His good work.

> **Love Is Not Rude or Self-Seeking** ♥ ♥ ♥
>
> **Not Rude:** Be courteous and kind. Gracious and using good manners.
>
> 1 Peter 4:8-10 "Above all, love each other deeply. Offer hospitality to one another without grumbling. Each of you should use whatever gift you have received to serve others....."
>
> **Not Self-Seeking:** Think of others first. Giving others first choice. Don't be greedy or selfish.
>
> 1 Corinthians 10:24 "No one should seek their own good, but the good of others."
>
> Acts 20:35 "....we must help the weak, remembering the words of the Lord Jesus himself said "It is more blessed to give than recieve."
>
> John 15:13 "Greater love has noone than this (love) to lay down one's life for one's own friends."
>
> Jesus said those words—and he did lay down his life. We can lay down our preferences and prefer others instead!

Love Is Not Easily Angered

It seems pretty straightforward that love cannot be expressed through human anger. It's a simple concept, but let's face it, we have all struggled in this area at times because of injustices, pride, offense, and selfishness (add in your own descriptor of something that can trigger anger).

Regardless of whether we are right or wrong, these can lead to anger if we give them room within our hearts. It doesn't matter if anger is openly and outwardly portrayed or bottled up in the heart—human anger is human anger. Our Father sees it all.

We struggle because we are human and flesh. There is hope! God already knows our weaknesses, and He can help the believing, humble, and contrite heart that brings that anger to Him.

Choose to give Him the battle. Choose to *humble* yourself before Him. Choose to ask for His direction on what to do. Choose to examine your own heart. Let God go before you and give Him the glory!

Friends, our time on earth is short. It's not about who is right or wrong; it's about the response we choose so that we can walk in the love God commands us to. Let's choose His way in truth and love.

Read the context of each scripture in **Matthew**, **Romans**, and **James**. Talk to our Father about this area in your own life and let Him do His good work. He is always faithful.

> LOVE IS NOT Easily Angered
>
> Ever find yourself getting easily angered with others, or a paticular person? Ask the Lord to help you see others through His eyes. Don't jump to conclusions. Ask questions and listen.
>
> Matthew 5:22 "But I tell you, that anyone who is angry with a brother or sister will be subject to judgement."
>
> Romans 15:2 "Each of us should please our neighbors for their good, to build them up."
>
> James 1:19-20 "My dear brothers & sisters, take note of this: Everyone should be quick to listen, slow to speak and slow to become angry, because human anger does not produce the righteousness that God desires."
>
> Friends, it's not about right or wrong. Give God the battle. It's about our response.

Love Keeps No Record of Wrongs

Forgiveness is a choice. It is the intentional and voluntary process of letting go of offense, negative emotions, and vengefulness, even if the wrong done to you or a loved one is an injustice.

Think about the amazing love our Savior, Jesus, has displayed in the work done on the cross so that we may have forgiveness of sins. He was beaten, bruised, broken, and ridiculed, yet He chose to walk in the will of His Father in love for us.

Let's admit it, sometimes forgiving is *hard*. We can give and receive forgiveness only when we first receive forgiveness from the Lord! His love enables us to forgive in love.

Let's pray: *Father, help us to receive Your love and give us forgiving hearts. Teach us what it means to fully forgive in love, even if a wrongful act seems worthy of reproach. We need You, Lord, and ask You today to help us love others the way You love us.*

Love Does Not Delight in Evil

Love does not delight in evil, so guard your heart! Guard what your eyes see and what your ears hear; protect your heart with His truth. My simple way of explaining this is that what goes into the heart is what will come out of your mouth and be seen in your actions.

"But those things which proceed out of the mouth come from the heart, and they defile a man" **(Matt. 15:18).**

Our faithful Father helps us to put off our old ways. He transforms us and helps us to be more like Him. He is faithful to do this by His Spirit in every way.

Read the context of all scriptures in **Matthew, Proverbs, Galatians, Ephesians, Philippians,** and **Isaiah** referenced below. Talk to our Father about your three personal questions. When you can answer all three, you are ready to move on.

> LOVE DOES NOT DELIGHT IN EVIL, IT REJOICES with THE TRUTH!
>
> Love does not delight in evil, so guard your heart! Guard what your eyes see and hear, protect your heart with His Truth.
>
> Matthew 15:18 "But the things that come out of a person's mouth come from the heart....."
>
> Can Also Reference: Matt. 5:29, Prov. 11:13, Gal. 6:1
>
> REJOICE! We are a new creation! REJOICE in the truth of who Christ is & who HE IS IN & Through You!
>
> Ephesians 4:22-25 "...Put of your old self, which is being corrupted by deceitful desires; to be made new in the attitude of your minds; and to put on the new self, created to be like God in true righteousness & holiness. Put off Falsehood & speak truth to your neighbor."
>
> Reference: Phil 1:18, Isa. 60:1

Love Always Protects

Our Lord is a mighty defender—our shield in this world.

"But You, O Lord, are a shield for me, / My glory and the One who lifts up my head" **(Ps. 3:3).**

When walking in His love for us, we will also walk in love for others, protecting the helpless and weak. We are also called to *protect our hearts* against the temptations of Satan, with the help of the Lord.

"Do not be anxious about anything, but in every situation, by prayer and petition, with thanksgiving present your requests to God. And the peace of God, which transcends all understanding, will guard your heart and your mind in Christ Jesus" **(Phil. 4:6–7 NIV).**

Finally, we are called to honor Christ and always be prepared to make a defense to anyone who asks us for a reason for the *hope* that is in us, by the power of Christ Jesus. Keep in mind that we are not called to defend God but to defend the testimony of the transformation that He has made in our lives **(**See **1 Peter 3:15–17).**

Let's pray: Lord, I ask for more of Your love to be reflected in my life; teach me to protect, guard, and defend Your way, not mankind's way in pride. I'm thankful, Lord, for all things, and I thank You for guarding our hearts and minds by Your Spirit in the midst of this world.

Love Always Trusts

What does it really mean to trust? Where does your hope lie? Have you ever tried to find peace by leaning on your own ability, your finances, your circumstances, other people, an amazing Insurance policy, or your investments? I've been there, and He has taught me over time to hold all the above with an open hand. It is all His and for His glory. He gives and takes away. Yes, the Lord can bless you and can use all these things in your life to provide, but they are *not* the source of hope or peace.

Romans 5:5 says, "And hope does not put us to shame because God's love has been poured out into our hearts through the Holy Spirit, who has been given to us."

You see, there is a desire that the Lord can spark in your heart as He is transforming you—a desire to want to walk a life in the love of God because love always trusts, believes, and hopes **(1 Cor. 13:7)**. He will pour it out in our lives!

In order to walk a life of love, trusting Him, I have to first *receive* His love—the true source of *hope*.

What does trust look like? Trust is looking to Him, believing, waiting, standing, resting, surrendering, praying, and not being fearful.

When we trust in love, He gives us strength, renewed hope, courage, perfect peace, delight, and joy. He makes our paths straight and guards our hearts and minds. He gives us life abundant, and we are helped.

He always works for the good of those who love and trust Him.

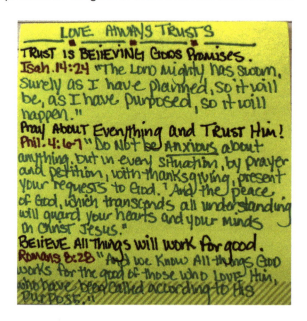

Love Always Hopes

1 Corinthian 13:7 continues to state that "Love always hopes." God is hope, and He wants to give us a future and hope.

Jeremiah 29:11 NKJV says "'For I know the thoughts that I think towards you says the Lord, thoughts of peace and not of evil, to give you a future and a hope."

Putting our hope in the Lord is a form of trust and faith.
My favorite definition of faith is in **Hebrews 11:1:** "Now faith is the substance of things *hoped* for, the evidence of things not seen" (my italicized emphasis).
As we hope in God, He pours out His love in our hearts by the power of the Holy Spirit **(***See* **Rom. 5:5)**.
I'm praying for *you*!

Lord, as we realize more fully the breadth and depth of what love really is, I pray over each reader and in this moment; You see each one, God: "May the God of hope fill you with all joy and peace in believing, that you may abound in hope by the power of the Holy Spirit" **(Rom. 15:13)**. *Amen.*

Read the context of each scripture referenced above and noted below. Talk to our heavenly Father about your three personal questions.

For His Glory | 83

Love Always Perseveres

I can remember a time at our church food pantry when our food order was canceled with only forty-eight hours' notice before the Saturday serve. Anywhere from 50–120 families usually came to receive. We could have handed out what little we had and sent cars home with empty hands that day. However, the Lord called us as a church body to pray. We prayed for His perfect provision; we prayed for His wisdom in what to do, and, within hours, calls and texts from the body of Christ started to come in. For the next two days, my husband, Brian, and I were up at the church receiving donations. Church families went through their personal pantries; some shopped and brought bulk items in; others were connected with other programs that had extra food and gave it to us; many gift cards came in. On the morning of the serve, every shelf, refrigerator, and freezer was full, and we had received enough provision for two serves! By God's grace and provision, we have never sent a family home empty-handed in almost fifteen years! All glory to You, God.

When we look to You, Lord, by Your Spirit, You help us to remain steadfast and calm in every circumstance. Perseverance is continued effort to do or achieve something, even when this is difficult or talks a long time (*Cambridge Dictionary*).

In every circumstance, the Lord's grace is sufficient! Choosing to press forward and pressing in to stand, trust, and pray is loving Him. This enables us to love others in every circumstance.

1 Peter 4:8 NIV says, "Above all, love each other deeply, because love covers a multitude of sins."

Are you or have you had to persevere through difficult circumstances? Talk to our Father about it. Talk to Him about your three personal questions and ask Him how He wants you to grow in this area.

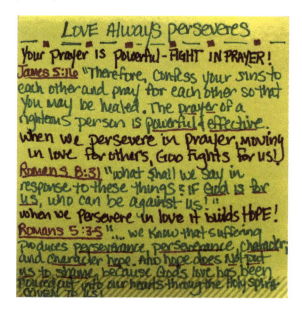

Love Never Fails

Did you ever think you could break down the descriptors of God's love from His Word in so many ways? I can't emphasize enough how important it is for us to have a heart revelation about receiving His love so that we can love others with His love.

Remember, we have to *choose* to love God; we have to *choose to receive* His love, and only then are we enabled to love others with His love. There is no other way.

Love is the most powerful gift; it is our greatest gift.

As we round out **1 Corinthians 13:1–8**, our last descriptor is Love *never* fails. It never fails! It doesn't just work on certain days of the week or in certain circumstances. When we choose to walk in love, it *never* fails. When we receive our Father's love, and we can respond in love, it *never* fails! Do you believe this?

We may not always see the results right away, but I can testify of the provision of His love: it has diffused anger, lifted spirits, brought comfort, offered peace (even as we humbled ourselves and prayed in difficult circumstances), planted joy in the hearts of people, and, most importantly, turned eyes to Jesus so that the Lord may be glorified in it—all for the sake of salvation for many.

By His Spirit, He does *all* this work. Allow the Lord to do His good work in you, whether you have known Him for a short time or for decades. He can always help you grow. Ask Him to give you a greater revelation of His love. It will be life-changing!

Let's pray: *Lord, help us to receive Your love so that we can walk in love. Help us in our responses right in our homes and let it spread to every area of our lives. It is our most powerful gift! Amen.*

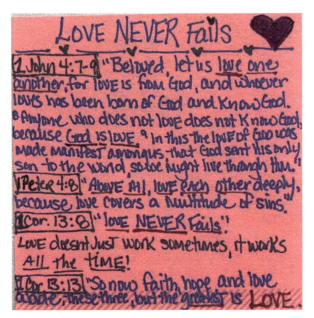

Seek the Lord

As believers in Christ, we are called to seek our Father's will first each day.

Matthew 6:33–34 NKJV says, "Seek ye first the Kingdom of God and His righteousness, and all these things shall be added to you. Therefore, do not worry about tomorrow, for tomorrow will worry about its own things. Sufficient for the day is its own trouble."

Today, people have busy lives, and it seems that as the advancement of technology increases, we just find more ways to do more things faster so that we can cram more into each day! Many of us are living in a society that encourages people to be what they want, do what they want, and be the masters of their own lives.

We have to choose to be set apart, to be different. We have to *determine* in our hearts to look to the Lord daily! We have to determine in our hearts to ask Him for His will. We have to choose to be obedient to His will for our lives.

Our Father is sitting at His table next to an open chair, waiting for us to come and sit with Him each day to talk to Him.

Seek Him today. If you don't have time each day to sit with Him, will you ask Him to show you when and how to commune with Him each day?

Let's pray: *Father, help us to focus on looking to You each day for Your way. Each time we pick up the responsibility of figuring out our own plans, remind us by Your Spirit, Lord, to hand it all back over to You. You created us for Your purpose Lord; help us to walk in it.*

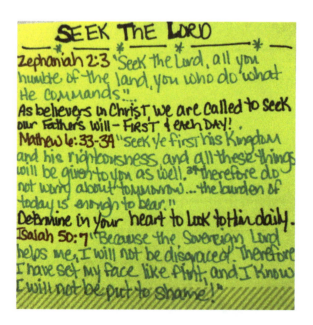

Wise in Heart

"Trust in the Lord with all your heart, and lean not on your own understanding; In all your ways acknowledge Him, And He shall direct your paths" **(Prov. 3:5–6 NKJV).**

    I love the instruction given in the book of Proverbs. He wants us to look to Him each day in all we do. The path He has for us may include difficult circumstances, tests or trials for our good, correction, and growth. Nonetheless, His love remains the same for us, and as we look to Him, He gives us the words to speak and the steps to take each day. He is always for our good. As we follow Him and grow in Him, He gives us His wisdom and writes it in our hearts.

    God can and will speak to you. He will give you wisdom for the plans He has for your life. He will give you wisdom for words you may need to say during an important conversation. He will give fresh *life* through the wisdom of His Word and bring joy to your heart.

    All you have to do is spend time with Him and ask. We thank you, Lord.

    Dive into the scriptures provided below. Read the context and talk to Him about your three personal questions.

> **WISE IN HEART**
>
> **Prov. 15:30-31** "Light in a messenger's eyes brings joy to the heart, and good news gives health to the bones. Whoever heeds life-giving correction will be at home among the wise."
>
> **Prov. 16:1** "To humans belong the plans of the heart, but from the Lord comes the proper answer of the tongue."
>
> **Prov. 16:9** "In their hearts humans plan their course, but the Lord establishes their steps."
>
> **Prov. 16:21** "The wise in heart are called discerning, and gracious words promote instruction."
>
> **Prov. 16:20** "Whoever gives heed to instruction prospers, and blessed is the one who trusts in the Lord."

Get Wisdom and Guard Your Heart

Psalm 119:105 says, "Your word is a lamp to my feet / And a light to my path."

God sent us His Word in Jesus Christ for the sake of salvation. He left us His Word in the form of the Bible as He knew it would bring life and instruction for each of us for all of time. How much He loves us!

Have you ever bought something that came with instructions you just threw away or stored and never read—maybe some type of appliance or gadget? (Confession . . . I'm totally thinking of my wall ovens and some snazzy gadgets in my toolbox.) It might seem intuitive enough to use, and maybe you can even take advantage of its primary purpose. However, maybe it was designed to do much more to help you with everyday tasks and activities, and you miss out on taking advantage of it because you don't know about the additional function it provides or when and how to apply it.

God's Word is similar, but the wisdom and instruction provided can lead to spiritual life or death if not understood and applied. Maybe we have a good understanding of its primary purpose; maybe we even believe, love, and have accepted Jesus Christ as our Lord and Savior. This is wonderful; however, there is *more*! There is more He wants to do in each of our lives to accomplish the full purpose He created each of us for.

This requires us to read His instructions for life. We need to understand the fullness of how we can walk each day in Him, request His help in making decisions, walk by the Spirit, and fully apply all the wisdom He has ensured to leave us in His word.

I don't know about you, but I don't want to miss out on one single thing our heavenly Father wants to do in me or through me. Let's get wisdom by spending time with Him and in His Word. Let's protect and guard it with all we are by asking for His help by His Spirit.

I can testify that it will change your life forever. Talk to Him about this.

> **Get Wisdom & Guard Your Heart**
>
> Proverbs 4:4-7 "Take hold of my words with all your heart; Keep my commands, and you will live. Get wisdom, get understanding; do not forget my words or turn from them. ⁶Do not forsake wisdom, and she will protect you; love her, and she will watch over you. ⁷The beginning of wisdom is this: Get wisdom though it costs all you have, get understanding."
>
> Proverbs 4:13 " Hold on to instruction, do not let it go; guard it well, for it is your life."
>
> Proverbs 4:23 " Above all else, guard your heart, for everything you do flows from it."
>
> Thank You Lord for Your word! The most perfect instruction & lamp for our feet. Thank You for Your Spirit whom helps us understand. Help us keep Your word in our heart & to guard it!

The Tongue Has the Power of Life or Death

Think about it: what we say has the power to bring life (to bless someone) or to bring death (wound the heart of someone or crush their sensitivity to the Spirit of God within them).

Oh, how we need the help of the Lord in using the tongue given us to speak! Help from the Lord, when we want and ask for it, starts with guarding our hearts, filling them with the Word of God, yielding them to Him, and letting them be filled by His Spirit.

God *always* sees our hearts. He knows what is in them. He knows what we let fill them. He always knows our every motive and intent. What we fill our hearts with will eventually come out of our mouths and be seen in our actions. Guard your heart.

"But those things that proceed out of the mouth come from the heart, and they defile a man" **(Matt. 15:18)**.

"He who answers a matter before he hears it, it is a folly and shame to him" **(Prov. 18:13)**.

"My dear brothers and sisters, take note of this: Everyone should be quick to listen, slow to speak and slow to become angry" **(James 1:19 NIV)**.

Read each scripture above and below and talk to the Lord about them. Let's ask the Lord to guard our hearts and help us by His Spirit when we speak in all circumstances.

> **The Tongue Has Power of Life or Death**
>
> Proverbs 18:21 "The tongue has the power of life and death, and those who love it will eat its fruit"
>
> Proverbs 10:20,21 "The tongue of the righteous is choice silver, the heart of the wicked of little value. 21 the lips of the righteous nourish many, but fools die for lack of sense."
>
> Proverbs 10:31 "From the mouth of the righteous comes the fruit of wisdom"......
>
> Mathew 15:18 "The things that come out of a persons mouth come from the heart"....
>
> James 3:17 "The (fruit of) wisdom that comes from heaven is first of all pure, then peace-loving, considerate, submissive, full of mercy and good fruit, impartial and sincere."

Foster Love in Love for Others

You can't love others with His love if you are walking in offense.

I know, that first line was very direct, friends. Will you let it impact your heart? Have you ever been offended—maybe by a loved one, a close friend, someone at work, or a stranger? *Release* it by laying it at God's feet. Harbored offense leads to bitterness, anger, and separation from others. In time, it influences your perspective in every aspect of life. It hurts God's calling on your life. It can lead to spiritual death.

I realize this can be hard once we realize we may have offended someone. I can recall a time a close friend, whom I still love today, was influenced by the world, chose a path not of the Lord, said horrible and accusing things about me, and broke off fellowship. I cried for weeks. I couldn't sleep. But in the night, as I cried out to God to ask Him for help, He simply and clearly said to me, "Offense separates close friends; do not repeat the matter." I learned that this is the heart of His Word in **Proverbs 17:9**.

As I determined in my heart not to harbor or allow offense (which is repeating the matter), the Lord helped me to lay down the hurt each day; sometimes, more than once a day. In time, the enemy no longer had the power to hurt my heart with that offense. I still love and pray for this friend today and trust God for restoration in His time.

Proverbs 27:21 NIV says, "The crucible for silver and the furnace for gold, but the Lord tests the heart."

Friends, we *will* be tested in this. We will have trying times, but He equips us and makes a way of escape through it all. He is always for our good and is faithful!

Let's ask Him to help us have clean hearts before Him so that we can love others!

Read each scripture in context and talk with Him.

The Lord Establishes Your Plans and Steps

Psalm 139:1–6 NKJV is about how the Lord searches us, knows us, perceives our thoughts from afar, and is familiar with *all* of our ways.

I love verse 6: "Such knowledge is too wonderful for me; It is high, / I cannot attain it."

God's ways are so much higher than our ways. His plans for us we may never fully understand until we walk in them, and He gives wisdom. This is true both when the walk seems easy and enjoyable and when it's difficult and wearisome. He will have His way, and He is always for the good of those who love Him.

Friends, we have to choose to abandon our own ways and choose His. We have to boldly and obediently step where He calls us to, even when we don't understand. How will we know His way? By the peace in our hearts. As we talk to Him and wait on Him, He will always confirm by His peace that passes all understanding.

Set your heart to be set apart for Him. Commit each day to Him and ask Him for His steps for you this day.

Read **Psalm 139** in full and the scriptures below in context. Talk to Him, surrender your plans, and ask for His.

The Lord Establishes Your Plans & Steps!

Proverbs 16:1-3 "To humans belong the plans of the heart, but from the Lord comes the proper answer of the tongue. Commit to the Lord whatever you do, and He will establish your plans."

There is an action required of us, to choose to commit (a form of trust) everything we do to Him and to His way.

Proverbs 16:9 "In their hearts humans plan their course, but the Lord establishes their steps."

Proverbs 19:21 "Many are the plans in a person's heart, but it is the Lord's purpose that prevails."

God always knows our heart, He always knows our motives, He always knows if we are doing things our own way! Give all things to Him and Trust Him, He will always have His way + will prevail!

Proverbs 19:23 "A person's steps are directed by the Lord. How can anyone understand their own way?"

Be Humble

I thank the Lord for His Son, Jesus—a beautiful example of humbleness. He entered the world as a little baby in lowly circumstances. He willingly walked this earth among men to have compassion and serve mankind. He willingly sacrificed His earthly life so we may have everlasting life.

If we want to walk humbly and in God's power, we have to first humble ourselves before Him. His Word says He opposes the proud **(James 4:6–7)**.

So how do we walk humbly? We have to *believe* who He is. We have to *believe* who He is *in* us. We have to surrender ourselves to Him and realize our human weakness. It is then that we can walk in His power, enabling us to love others with His wisdom and love.

Let's pray: *Father, give me a heart of compassion, servanthood, and love for Your glory. Help us each to remember, Lord, that as we humble and surrender ourselves before You, we acknowledge our own weakness in our flesh. Thank you, Lord, for the strength You give us by Your Spirit. Amen.*

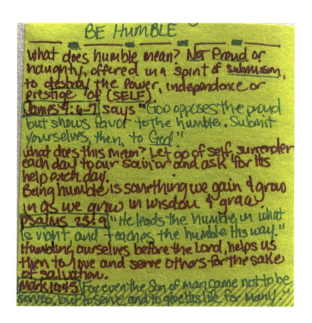

Loving God Enables Us to Love Others

The Lord's instruction is always given by perfect design and order.

For example, in **Matthew 22:37–39 NKJV**, He says, "'You shall love the Lord your God with all your heart with all your soul, and with all your mind.' This is the first and great commandment. And the second is like it: 'You shall love your neighbor as yourself.'"

Note that we must *first love Him* with all our hearts, souls, and minds. We can then *receive* His love, which *enables* us to love others.

If we tried to reverse it, if we tried to love others on our own without the Father's love, we would fail. Our love alone lacks His power and it becomes impossible in our own strength. And we have learned that His love never fails!

Likewise, perfect instruction was given to the disciples in **Acts** and applies to us today.

Read **Acts 1:4–8**. We are called to

1. *Wait* on the Lord and the gift of His power by His Holy Spirit.
2. *Receive* His power when the Holy Spirit comes upon us.
3. *Go* and *be witnesses* to the ends of the earth.

Trying to witness without first waiting on Him and His leading and asking for help by His Spirit would yield a powerless, unfruitful ministry.

Let us pray: *Lord God, help us to love You with all we are. Help us to receive Your love so that we may walk in Your love toward others. Help us to be led by You, to walk in Your power so that we may share the gospel message. Stir up a desire in our hearts, Lord, to be used by You and for Your glory. Amen.*

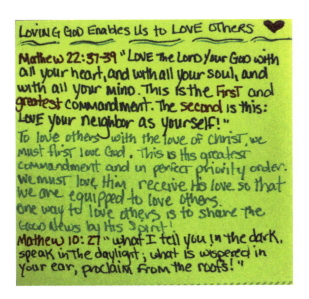

The Lord God Will Keep You

Read **Psalm 121:5–8**. The Lord is your keeper; what a promise!

Look up the word *keep* and its various definitions. These are some of my favorites: in charge, in control. He is the provider of all needs, He preserves, and He is a refuge.

The Lord God keeps and watches over you *today*.

He keeps and watches over you *all of your days* to come.

"'For I know the plans I have for you,' declares the Lord, 'plans to prosper you and not to harm you, plans to give you hope and a future'" **(Jer. 29:11 NIV)**.

"Trust in the Lord forever. For in YAH, the LORD, is everlasting strength" **(Isa. 26:4 NKJV)**.

He keeps and has prepared for you *the way* of eternal days with Him and everlasting life through Him.

Rest in this promise *all* your days.

Meditate on each scripture and talk to Him about your three personal questions. Consider journaling your responses.

> **The Lord God will KEEP you**
>
> Psalm 121:7-8 "The Lord God will keep you from all harm He will watch over your life; the Lord will watch over your coming and going both now and forevermore."
>
> What does "KEEP" mean here? He is in charge, in control, He is provider of all needs, He is a refuge.
>
> 1 John 5:18 "We know that anyone born of God does not continue to sin; the One who was born of God keeps them safe, and the evil one cannot harm them."
>
> REST IN HIM. TRUST IN HIM.

God Will Uphold Us

God, our King of Kings and Lord of Lords, has *all* authority, and He gave that to His Son, Jesus. I'm full of awe and wonder at the thought that He lives within us!

I'm reminded of a time in the corporate workplace when I'd heard of a new Christian life group starting to form in our office out in California. In my heart, I knew I was called to be connected in some way but I was very cautious as I wanted to understand the heart of the ministry and ensure it was our Lord's will. Was this a ministry that focused on our one mighty God, who gave His Son, Jesus, to die on the cross for our sins and sent His Holy Spirit to live within us? Did I have the time? I worked an 8 to 5 corporate job in an executive leadership role. The drive was an hour away, and, most importantly, my heart was in ministry for our Lord twenty-four seven, and that meant most nights and weekends were spent doing something for Him in our local church. I reached out to connect and learn more, and then my husband and I waited and prayed.

It wasn't but a few weeks after that my husband shared that he felt peace in his heart and that I should connect and be part of this workplace ministry in some way. Just a day or so later, I received a call from one of our senior leaders who said, "Darlene, we know you love God. Associates in San Antonio are hearing about the Christian life group, and over a hundred have signed up so far this week. Can you help sponsor our San Antonio group?" I thought, "Okay, Lord. I hear you! I'll do it. But how, Lord, can a Christ-centered group exist and move by Your Spirit within the confines of a secular workplace? Can we be true to who You are within us?"

The Lord spoke **Isaiah 41:10 NIV** to my heart: "So do not fear, for I am with you; do not be dismayed, for I am your God. I will strengthen you and help you; I will uphold you with My righteous right hand."

My heavenly Father *did* strengthen me. He gave all help and wisdom and upheld me in every way. He did miracles in the hearts of many in the workplace! Through Bible studies, prayer times, devotionals, and worship events, God raised up His people and connected hundreds in several offices across the globe. Eventually, He called me not only to serve and lead the San Antonio group, but to serve, unite, and lead the global group as well.

After years of schooling, earning degrees, working in the professional workplace, and other accomplishments, I'm most privileged and thankful *by far* to have the opportunity to stand for Him in the workplace in this way. It will always be my favorite thing and the highlight of my corporate career.

The One who has all authority over the earth is the One who helps you and holds you by the hand in all He calls you to and equips you for.

> God will uphold us with His
>   righteous right hand!
> ———*———*———*———
> Isaiah 41:10 So do not fear, for I am with you; do not be dismayed, for I am your God. I will strengthen you and help you; I will uphold you with my righteous right hand.
> Isaiah 41:13 For I am the Lord your God who takes hold of your right hand and says to you, Do not fear; I will help you.
> Luke 20:42-43 The Lord said to my Lord: "Sit at my right hand until I make your enemies a footstool for your feet."
> The ONE who has all authority over the earth is the ONE who helps you and holds you by the hand! What A Promise!

Train for a Crown That Lasts Forever

Let's think about Paul's example where he compares this life we live to a runner competing in a race.

Read **1 Corinthians 9:24–26.** Paul's example points us to

1. Give everything for Him.
2. Be disciplined with a determination to be rooted and grounded in Him. We train by spending our time with Him.
3. Remember, our reward is eternal life!
4. Do all things with His purpose!

Lord, help our legacy on this earth testify of how we love You and show Your love! Let us all desire to have a heart like Paul's in **2 Timothy**:

I have fought the good fight, I have finished the race, I have kept the faith. Now there is in store for me the crown of righteousness, which the Lord, the righteous judge, will award to me on that day—and not only to me but also to all who have longed for His appearing. **(2 Tim. 4:7–8 NIV)**

Talk to our heavenly Father about your life, the plan, and the race He has already set before you. Talk to Him about your three personal questions.

Keep in Step with the Spirit

In both **Matthew 22:37–40** and **Mark 12:29–31**, the Lord instructs us to love Him with all our hearts, minds, and souls and then to love our neighbors as ourselves.

How? He instructs us to walk by the Spirit which will produce fruit of the Spirit. I love the encouragement in **Galatians 5:25 ESV**: "If we live by the Spirit, let us also *keep in step* with the Spirit" (my emphasis).

What does it mean to keep in step with the Holy Spirit? Picture a marching band moving together in perfect synchronization. It means we walk in perfect alignment, timing, and unity with our Father by His Spirit.

This is freedom!
We are *free* in Christ Jesus. Because His Spirit lives within us, we can walk *with* Him. When we walk by the Spirit, we do not gratify the desires of our weak, human flesh. This produces the fruit of the spirit as described in **Galatians 5:22**.

Let's pray: Lord I want to walk daily in Your way. I desire to keep in step with Your Spirit. I confess my weakness, Lord, and that I need Your help to do so. I thank You that I am free in You. Amen.

> **Keep in step with the Spirit**
> Galatians 5:25 "Since we live by the Spirit, let us keep in step with the Spirit."
> In Galatians 5:13, Paul says "You, my brothers and sisters are called to be free." "To serve one another in love."
> How? Galatians 5:16 says "So I say, walk by the Spirit, and you will not gratify desires of the flesh."
> This produces the fruit of the Spirit as described in Galatians 5:22.
> So Galatians 5:25 says "let us keep in step with the Spirit". What does this mean? Think of an army marching or a marching band. It means to walk in perfect alignment, timing, and in perfect unity with."
> This is freedom.

I Bow My Knees to the Father

I love the picture that comes to mind with the statement Paul made in **Ephesians 3:14–19**. Read the scripture and the context of the chapter to understand why he said it.

Of all the promises or resolutions we try to make in our lives, I think the most valuable would be to resolve to *pray*; to bow our knees before our heavenly Father and ask Him what our focus should be, for His glory. We can seek His direction, be strengthened, and share our deepest thoughts and concerns with Him.

Prayer is a vital source of life and a weapon! It immediately helps us connect with our King of Kings and enter into His presence. We *need it*. Think about it: when our physical bodies are sick, we care for them, nurse them to health, maybe see a physician, and give them medication and rest. If our spiritual lives are lacking and sick, do we give this vital life the same care and attention? Prayer and communion with our Lord will bring life and health to our spiritual lives. It allows us to rest fully in Him regardless of our circumstances.

Talk to our Father. Ask the Holy Spirit to help you pray; ask Him when you should pray. Ask Him to help you be obedient to pray when He brings it to mind, and find rest in Him. Talk to Him about your three personal questions.

> I bow My Knees to The Father....
>
> Ephesians 3:14-19 "For This reason I bow my knees to the Father of our Lord Jesus Christ, from whom the whole family in heaven and earth is named, that He would grant you, according to the riches of His glory, to be strengthened with might through His Spirit in the inner man, that Christ may dwell in your hearts through faith; that you, being rooted and grounded in love, may be able to comprehend with all the saints what is the width and length and depth and height—to know the love of Christ which passes knowledge; that you may be

Ask the Father to Teach You to Fast and Pray

The deepest desire of the disciples in **Luke 11:1** is wonderful: they wanted to ask Jesus to teach them to pray. They were walking on this earth at the same time as Jesus; they could have watched others, copied them, or mimicked them, but they wanted to learn directly from Jesus. In love, Jesus's response was immediate.

Sometimes, we may think we know how to fast and pray, but the moment we think this, we limit what God wants to do! Fasting to pray is a sign of humbling ourselves before the Lord—a decrease of self so He can increase in us.

A fast can look different for different people; how and what you fast and for how long can be different at various times when He calls you to pray. Ask Him, and He will help you.

Let's not assume we know how; instead, let's ask the Lord to teach us something new about fasting and praying so that He may do a *new* thing!

> Ask our Father to teach you to Fast & Pray
>
> Luke 11:1 "One day Jesus was Praying in a certain place. When He finished, one of His disciples said to Him, "Lord, teach us to pray, just as John taught his disciples."
>
> The heart desire of this disciple is precious! He had a yearning to learn from our Savior. Lord, give us this heart's desire!
>
> Jesus' response was immediate.
>
> Luke 11:2 "He said to them, "When you pray, say: ......"
>
> I love the heart of our Savior. When we ask for His help, His response is immediate!!

Prayer and Fasting in Your Secret Place

God sees us in our secret places. These secret places can be anywhere the Lord draws us unto Him: a special room, our cars, a walking path, anywhere the Lord draws us unto Him and we obediently go to seek His face and to talk to Him.

It is not just about *where* we go:

- He sees our hearts.
- He sees our humbleness before Him.
- He sees our acts of worship before Him.
- He hears us.
- He sees our obedience.

Prayer and fasting in secret is a picture of humbling ourselves before God (not doing things as if for mankind). It is an act of worship rewarded by the Lord and His promises!

Read the context of each scripture below. Talk to our Lord about how He wants you to grow in your prayer time with Him. Talk to Him about your three personal questions and let Him speak to your heart.

> Prayer & Fasting in your Secret Place
>
> What Jesus says About Prayer:
> Mathew 6:6
> His Instruction: "But when you pray, go into your room, close the door and pray to your Father, who is unseen……
> His Promise: Then your Father, who sees what is done in secret, will reward you."
>
> What Jesus says About Fasting:
> mathew 6:17-18
> His Instruction: "But when you fast, put oil on your head and wash your face, so that it will not be obvious to others that you are fasting, but only to your Father, who is unseen……
> His Promise: and your Father, who sees what is done in secret, will reward you."

Bear One Another's Burdens

Fasting and praying is not just something we do for a time; it should be something we do whenever God calls us as we walk with Him.

He calls us to love Him with all our hearts, minds, and souls; seeking His face through fasting and prayer is part of it. Loving Him enables us to love others, and since God calls us to love our neighbors as ourselves, interceding for others is part of it! Part of loving others in Christ is carrying the burdens of others in prayer, laying them at the feet of our Lord, and *leaving them there*. We do this not in our own strength but by His Spirit, fighting alongside others in the body of Christ.

To intercede means to intervene between parties with the view of *reconciling* differences—to mediate or go between. Go ahead and look up a few definitions. I love this picture! We are called to *go* to our Father *on behalf* of those we are called by Him to love! Thank you, Lord, for the privilege of this calling and weapon of prayer.

"Bear one another's burdens and so fulfill the law of Christ" **(Gal. 6:2 NKJV)**.

Let's pray: *Father, help us, by Your Spirit, to pray. Help our hearts understand what it means to fast and how and when You may call us to this sacrifice and humbling of self before You. Place others in our hearts and minds to pray for and to lay at Your feet. I trust You, God, to move in Your faithful might and power according to Your will. Amen.*

> **Bear one anothers burdens**
> Galatians 6:2 "Bear one anothers burdens and so fulfil the law of Christ."
> What is the law of Christ?
> Mathew 22:37 "Love the LORD your God with all your heart, mind and soul." and second 39. "You shall love your neighbor as yourself."
> Part of loving others in Christ is carrying the burdens of others in love. Not in our strength, but fighting in prayer alongside and for others in the body of Christ.
> 1 Timothy 2:12 "Therefore I exhort first of all that supplications, prayers, intercessions, and giving thanks be made for all men....."

Anticipate the Victory

During the pandemic, our church body fasted and prayed together for the body of Christ. The first month, we fasted together for twenty-one days. After that, we fasted and prayed together as a body for the first three days of each month. Our heart was to pray first for the church body as a whole, then for each other, and to seek Him for our personal requests last.

Remember, what you fast is between you and the Lord, and each individual's health should always be considered. Our Father knows our needs, and He can see our hearts humbling before Him. Whether it be one meal, two meals, no meals, liquid only, or a specific type of food or drink, each of us should ask Him how and when we should fast and pray.

The Lord moved mightily as we prayed. I started to journal the requests of others and, over time, began to see how He moved and answered in many ways. Our heavenly Father may not answer in the ways we think He will, but He will *always* answer!

How important it is to *believe* as we fast and pray! Walk in *belief* and *trust*. The action of believing is *so* powerful. Friends, you either believe or you don't; there is no in-between. Resolve to believe and trust Him as He will continue to move no matter how small or big our requests are before Him. Look to the Lord with the expectation of His goodness. Anticipate the *victory* in the Lord!

> **Anticipate The Victory!**
>
> Mathew 21:22 "If you believe, you will receive whatever you ask for in Prayer." In this story of Jesus withering the fig tree, Jesus taught the disciples that if they had faith and did not doubt, miracles could happen! All according to the will of God and for His glory.
>
> James 5:16 "Therefore confess your sins to each other and pray for each other so that you may be healed. The prayer of a righteous person is powerful and effective!"
>
> Psalms 145:14-15 "The Lord upholds all who fall, and raises up all who are bowed down. The eyes of all look expectantly to you, and you give them food in due season."

Seeing Others through God's Eyes

"For the Lord does not see as man sees; for man looks at the outward appearance, but the Lord looks at the heart" **(1 Sam. 16:7)**.

In reading the context of this scripture, you will find that God spoke these words as he sent Samuel to the house of Jesse. God provided Himself a king among Jesse's sons; Samuel was sent to anoint and appoint this new king. All of Jesse's sons passed before Samuel, and it wasn't until the youngest, David, that the Lord spoke and said he was the one to anoint.

Have you ever judged or made an assumption about someone based on superficial details such as how they look, dress, or their first response toward you? We must get to know others and build relationships to better understand people and their hearts. We must take the time to really see them.

Our heavenly Father *knows* and *sees* every person He has created—past, present, and future—both the believer and non-believer. God sees our hearts as worthy of love.

I have, at times, asked the Lord to help me see others with His eyes. Not in an irreverent way by any means, but in a way that does not make assumptions or cast judgment based on what my physical eyes observe. I'm asking the Lord to help me see others with His love and to have the discernment to get to know others.

Is there anyone in your life you need to ask the Lord to help you see with His eyes?
Let's pray: *Lord, by Your Spirit, help us to move and to walk in love toward others. Help us take the time to understand their hearts and to point both the unbeliever and believer to You. Amen.*

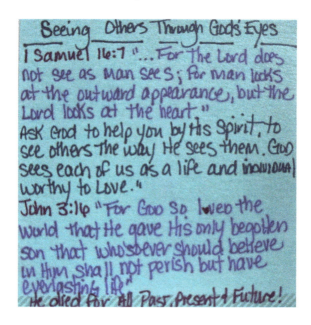

Seeing Circumstances through God's Eyes

Do you ever get discouraged, frustrated, or confused about why you are in a difficult circumstance? Ask the Lord to help you see this difficult circumstance through His eyes.

Second Corinthians 4:17 says, "For our light affliction, which is but for a moment, is working for us a far more exceeding and eternal weight of glory."

Let's be real: If we are walking in unbelief, as unbelievers unrepentant of sin, or if we are making decisions with the wrong motives and in our own strength, there are tough consequences we may have to live through! God's mercy is always available to those who turn to Him.

However, the believer walking humbly before the Lord and seeking His heart can trust Him as the Master Potter. He controls the potter's wheel—the circumstances of our lives! He is always in complete control. Whatever season you are in, thank Him, seek His face, and ask to see your circumstance through His eyes. Ask Him *what* He wants to do through it rather than *why* it is happening. Take heart: what is now a light affliction is doing its work for an eternal weight of glory!

Read each scripture in context and talk to Him about your three personal questions. He will meet you right where you are.

> **Seeing Circumstances Through God's Eyes**
>
> Ephesians 1:11 "In Him we have obtained an inheritance, having been predestined according to the purpose of him who works all things according to the council of His will..."
>
> God has a perfect Purpose for us, and an everlasting plan for us - For His Glory!
>
> Jeremiah 29:11 "For I know the plans I have for you, declares the Lord, plans for welfare and not for evil, to give you a future and a hope."
>
> For the believer, God is THE MASTER POTTER AND IN CONTROL of that Potter's wheel! The circumstances of our lives, GOOD AND BAD - But all For His greater glory!
>
> Hebrews 3:1 WE HAVE A Heavenly CALLING - FOR

Abide in Christ

"Abide in Me, and I in you. As the branch cannot bear fruit of itself, unless it abides in the vine, neither can you, unless you abide in Me" **(John 15:4)**.

What does it mean to abide in Christ? The definition of the word *abide* has been added to over centuries; however, if we look at the Hebrew and Greek meanings, it helps us understand the instructions of Jesus in **John 15**:

Yashab (Hebrew)—To sit, to remain, to dwell.

Meno (Greek)—To stay, to remain.

Our Savior instructs us to remain and live in Him as He lives in us so that He can live *through* us in our lives!

The Lord reminded me of this as our world was brought to its knees through the pandemic. He reminded me to be on my knees resting in His presence. Even in the midst of lockdowns and isolation, I was not alone; He was still moving by His Spirit for His glory and purpose. He is always just looking for a willing vessel who abides in Him.

Let us pray: *Father, help us to pray and to ask for Your help. You, Lord, are the source of our strength, wisdom, and healing—all that we need! Apart from You, Lord, we can do nothing. Thank you, Lord, that You are our place of rest as we abide in You. We are never alone in Your presence. Amen.*

Talk to our Lord about your three personal questions and ask Him to speak to you about abiding in Him.

> **Abide in Christ**
> What does Abide mean? To Stay, Remain, to sit or to dwell.
> John 15:4-5 "Abide in me, and I in you. As the branch cannot bear fruit by itself, unless it abides in the vine, neither can you, unless you abide in me. 5 I am the vine; you are the branches. Whoever abides in me, and I in him, he it is that bears much fruit, for apart from me you can do nothing."
> Father, help us to Abide, to rest and live in you! Use us Lord to bear much fruit for your Kingdom and to be a light for You.
> Mathew 11: 28-29 "Take my yoke upon you, and learn from me, for I am gentle and lowly in heart, and you will find REST for your souls."

Rejoice, Be Patient, and Pray

"Rejoicing in hope, patient in tribulation, continuing steadfastly in prayer" **(Rom. 12:12)**.

In the book of Romans, Paul instructed believers on what the character of Christ should look like through our lives. In times of difficulty and tribulation, we earnestly need the help of the Holy Spirit to respond with Christlike character in the moment and to be His witnesses for His glory throughout the day.

As we are living through a global pandemic, unprecedented natural disasters, crumbling politics, wars, and rumors of wars, we *need* the help of the Holy Spirit to walk in Christ's love with boldness and confidence.

Praise our sovereign heavenly Father who is in control of *all* things. Praise Him for His promise of pouring out His Holy Spirit even more in the last days; we need Him! Praise Him, for He foretold that in the world we will have tribulation, but He has overcome the world!

Let's pray: *Father, help us to walk in Your word. Help us to rejoice in hope, be patient in tribulation, and be constant in prayer. Help us to boldly walk in Your trust and be a light for Your glory. You made us for such a time as this! Amen.*

"Now may the God of hope fill you with all joy and peace in believing, that you may abound in hope, through the power of the Holy Spirit" **(Rom. 15:13)**.

Read each scripture in the context of the chapter and book and talk to Him about your three personal questions.

> REJOICE, Be Patient and Pray!
> Romans 12:12 says "Rejoice in hope, be patient in tribulation, be constant in prayer."
> Romans 15:13 "Now may the God of hope fill you with all joy and peace in believing, that ye may abound in hope, through the power of the Holy Ghost."
> Be patient, He is in complete control!
> John 16:33 "I have said these things to you, that in me you may have peace. In the world you will have tribulation. But Take heart; I have overcome the world."
> Pray and He will give you Peace!
> Philippians 4:6-7 "Do not be anxious about anything, but in everything by prayer and supplication with thanksgiving, let your requests be made known to God. And peace of God will guard your hearts and minds

Let Your Life Be a Testimony

We are the hands and feet of Jesus! I listened to a pastor recently who said, "We are God's plan A for this generation, in this time!" Do you believe that you are His plan, His hands, and His feet at this time for His purpose?

The Lord calls us to love Him with all our hearts, minds, and souls, and to love others **(Matt. 22:37–39)**. The Lord *made* us for this! He made us to be witnesses and testimonies to others. That is our part, to be His hands and feet, and we are His plan A for our generation, in our time, right where He has placed us. God will do the rest, and He will bring the increase. God will draw people unto Himself. I *love* this.

John 6:44–45 says, "No one can come to Me unless the Father who sent Me draws him; and I will raise him up at the last day. It is written in the prophets, 'And they shall all be taught by God.' Therefore, everyone who has heard and learned from the Father comes to Me."

Do you see the *freedom* and *joy* we have in our part—to love others, share the good news, and let our lives be a testimony? God does the rest!

He draws. He teaches. By His Son, Jesus, He saves!

Praise the Lord, and, friend, *go* and let your life be a witness unto Him. You are plan A, and He created you for such a time as this!

Study the context of the scriptures provided and talk to our Lord about your three personal questions. If you feel excitement bubbling up and drawing on your heart right now, He's calling you by His Spirit!

The Life of Jesus in Us

"Always carrying about in the body the dying of the Lord Jesus, that the *life* of Jesus also may be manifested in our body. For we who live are always delivered to death for Jesus's sake, that the life of Jesus also may be manifested in our mortal flesh" **(2 Cor. 4:10–11 my emphasis)**

As believers in Christ, what does it mean to be "delivered to death for Jesus's sake"? It is about dying to self, *surrendering* everything we are to His will and way.

Galatians 2:20 ESV says, "I have been crucified with Christ; it is no longer I who live, but Christ who lives in me. And the *life* I now live in the flesh I live by faith in the Son of God, who loved me and gave Himself for me."

Our dying to self leads to beautiful treasure—the *life* of Jesus Christ *in* us! The power of God by His Spirit resides in us. We have the *power* of God within us! Do you believe that? We have to believe it to walk in it as He leads. He lives in and through us. Help us, Lord, not to take this for granted. What a promise and what a wonderful gift of life because our Savior willingly gave His own for us.

As you go about each day living life, how does God want to show His power for His glory through you? He can do it right where He has you: in your home, at work, in the church body, at the grocery store, at the gas pump, anywhere He calls your hands and feet to go. Ask Him to help you live a life of His power for His glory. Believe it.

> **The Life of Jesus in us!**
>
> 2 Corinthians 4:7 "But we have this treasure in earthen vessels, that the excellence of the power may be of God and not of us."
>
> 2 Corinthian 4:10-11 "always carrying about in the body the dying of the Lord Jesus, that the life of Jesus also may be manifested in our body. For we who live are always delivered to death for Jesus' sake, that the life of Jesus also may be manifested in our mortal flesh."

Search Me, Oh God

Have you ever paused, spoken to the Lord, and asked Him to search your heart? It is *transforming*. Think about it: God made you, He already *knows* you. He knows your every thought and your every motive of the heart. He already knows the plans He has for you. He is the Master Potter who has the vision of the vessel He is molding and shaping.

So, you might be thinking, *If He knows all this, why is it so important to ask Him to search our hearts?* In the midst of God's omnipotence and omniscience, He wants something of us: He wants a relationship with us, and He wants us to desire *Him*. Most importantly, He wants us to *ask* Him to search us, to search our hearts, and to change us by His Spirit to be more like Him. He wants us to ask Him, not so that He can see, but so that *we* can see, therefore giving us the opportunity to yield to His transformative hand.

Read each scripture and talk to Him about your three personal questions. Ask Him over the next several days to search your heart, and let Him speak to you. Consider writing down what He brings to your heart and mind.

His Word Is Written on Your Heart

God's Word searches our hearts, shines light in the darkness, and waters our souls—it transforms. By the power of the Holy Spirit, it leads us into rest.

Read each scripture below in **Hebrews, Proverbs,** and **Psalms.**

Hebrews 4 says,

Let us therefore be diligent to enter that rest, lest anyone fall according to the same example of disobedience. For the word of God is living and powerful, and sharper than any two-edged sword, piercing even to the division of soul and spirit, and of joints and marrow, and is a discerner of the thoughts and intents of the heart. **(Hebrews 4:11–12)**

> His word *transforms*. Treasure His commands *within* you, *seek* to be in His word with your whole heart, and His word will be written in your heart.

Talk to your heavenly Father about being in His word and walking in it. Talk to Him about what it means to rest in His word and who He is, no matter your circumstances.

> **His word is written on your Heart**
>
> Proverbs 7:1-3 "My son (daughter), keep my words, and treasure my commands within you. ² Keep my commands and live, and my law as the apple of your eye. ³ Bind them on your fingers; write them on the tablet of your heart."
>
> The word of God is powerful and by His Spirit transforms the heart. Dive in with your whole heart!
>
> Psalm 119:10-11 "With my whole heart I have sought You; Oh let me not wander from Your commandments! Your word I have hidden in my heart, that I might not sin against You."

You Are His Special Treasure

During the worldwide pandemic, I've had more time to enjoy the outdoors and just sit in the presence of the Lord. I'm so thankful for this gift. I'm reminded of the wonderful care He takes in every living thing. With the change of scenery, I've noticed cardinals, red robins, doves, a woodpecker, and multiple varieties of hummingbirds all living in the same oak tree next to my back porch. Yesterday, I was visited by a flock of black-bellied whistling ducks. I never noticed them before or even knew how to identify them all; in the busyness of life, I never had time to sit on the back porch! By God's grace, I'm learning with His help and in delight. The detail and beauty of each species is so amazing! In it, I see the beauty and care of the Lord's hand.

It reminds me of the scripture in **Matthew 6:26:** "Look at the birds of the air, for they neither sow nor reap nor gather into barns; yet your heavenly Father feeds them. Are you not more valuable than they?"

Friends, I'm reminded that as His children, we are His very special treasures, and He wonderfully cares for and looks over us.

Read the context of scripture in **Matthew, Romans,** and **Deuteronomy** and seek His heart for you and your family.

> **You Are His Special Treasure**
> Romans 8:14 "For as many as are led by the spirit of God, these are sons of God."
> Romans 8:16 "The Spirit Himself bears witness with our spirit that we are children of God...."
> As a child of God, a daughter of the Most High King, a son of the Most High King – you are His Special Treasure.
> Deuteronomy 14:2 "For you are a holy people to the Lord your God, and the Lord has chosen you to be a people for Himself, a special treasure above all the peoples who are on the face of the earth."

Be Wise with Your Time

We have recently experienced a period of complete reevaluation of every activity that takes up our time. As a result of the global pandemic, we have had to rethink what we do, how we do it, when we do it, who we can spend time with, and even how many people we can be around at one time. The sickness and loss are heartbreaking, and I pray for all those who already have or may yet walk through that difficulty. I've personally recovered from COVID-19, and my heart has compassion for anyone who does get it.

However, I'm also thankful for the required pause on life in the midst of our whirlwind society. It has been yet another reminder of how short our time is here on this earth. I want to live and breathe every moment of it for His purpose and glory. I don't want to miss one miracle in which He may use me as His instrument. Writing this very devotional (and book) is a miracle! I never set out to be an author! Only He knew. I want to be a good steward of how I spend my time, doing the things He calls me to.

The Lord calls us to be watchful and consider carefully how we spend our time! Only God knows our last day on this earth, and only He knows the day of Christ's return!

Matthew 24:36 says, "But of that day and hour no one knows, not even the angels of heaven, but My Father only."

God wants us to be wise with our time and to walk according to His purpose each day! Our days are numbered, and our Lord has already established the work of our hands.

Read the context of the scriptures listed in **Matthew, Ephesians,** and **Psalms**. Talk to Him.

Let's pray: *Father, help us to be wise with our time and to carefully consider how we spend it. Help us to ask You how to walk through each day. Help us walk with You, Lord. Thank You for Your faithfulness!*

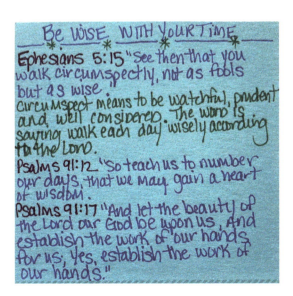

Sound Your Trumpet

For a recent National Day of Prayer, I was privileged and blessed to lead and participate in a time of gathering to pray in the workplace. Although it had to be done virtually due to the pandemic and working from home, associates across the United States and London joined to pray. In preparing my own heart, I asked the Lord for a word. Many of our associates had fear and sorrow from loss or sickness; some were lonely, and some were very overwhelmed by the change in family dynamics. Only He could meet the needs of His people. He quickly and simply responded, "Sound your trumpet!"

Sound your trumpet? I'll never forget His voice. What did He mean by this? In **Numbers 10,** the Lord instructed Moses to make two silver trumpets to be used for calling the people together and directing the movement of the camps. The Lord reminded me of the importance of gathering in His name, fighting in prayer, and rejoicing thankfully in His victory.

Our heavenly Father, by His Spirit, can help us recognize, respond to, rely on, and rejoice in the calling to gather together as the body of Christ to fight in prayer:

1. **Recognize** when it's time to go to war in prayer.
2. **Respond** to the call to action.
3. **Rely** on our Lord God to supply our spiritual and physical needs in the fight.
4. **Rejoice** in our faithful King who will bring the victory!

And always be *ready*, He may use *you* to "sound your trumpet" and gather His people.

Stand on the Anchor

I'll never forget the time my husband and I went saltwater fishing off the coast of Texas with my dad. We spent a beautiful morning in the bay on the boat, but in the early afternoon, we suddenly saw dark clouds looming on the horizon. Within minutes, the wind picked up and was strong enough to blow our boat against the current. There had not been a forecast of a storm or rain that day, and caught by surprise, we were too far out in the bay to get back home in time to avoid the storm. There was a small sandbar-like island, and the wind, current, and waves were quickly blowing our boat toward the shore. My father suddenly said, "Drop anchor! Get into the water, and Brian, go stand on the anchor! Everyone HOLD FAST!"

For a moment I thought my dad was *crazy*! We might drown! (The water was shallow enough for us to literally stand on the anchor by the way.) By then it was dark and raining so hard it hurt. As lightning flashed and the wind blew, the waves picked up. I jumped in, afraid.

However, the water was warm. It shielded us from the stinging rain, and as we stood on and held fast to that anchor and rope, we were held firmly in place. The wind blew a tide in that pushed several other boats to the shore. The storm passed within ten minutes, but as the wind and waves ceased and the tide went back out, all those boats were stranded on dry land! Because we and our boat were safe, we spent the afternoon helping to pull those other boats back into the water.

Stand on and *hold fast* to our Anchor, Jesus Christ. Our Lord God and His Son, Jesus, will help you weather any storm and avoid shipwreck, equipping you with the grace and strength to show others His unfailing love.

Everything and all things for His glory!

> **STAND ON THE ANCHOR**
>
> Hebrews 6:17-19 "Thus God, determining to show more abundantly to the heirs of promise the immutability of His counsel, confirmed it by an oath, that by two immutable things, in which it is impossible for God to lie, we might have strong consolation who have fled for refuge to lay hold of the hope set before us. This Hope we have as an anchor of the soul, both sure and steadfast, and which enters the presence behind the veil."
>
> Jesus is the One who has gone before us! We are called to stand firm in the promise and Hope of whom Christ is for us! He is our firm foundation in every circumstance. When in the storm hold fast to your firm Anchor.

Healing Starts within Our Hearts

My heart can't help but cry out about how our world, nation, and people need God's healing and rest! We truly live in a time in which good in the Lord is made to look evil, and evil is made to look good. Our Father knows and sees! I pray for repentance and revival within our nation before our Savior's return, and I realize the healing starts right within my own heart.

"If My people who are called by My name will humble themselves, and pray and seek My face, and turn from their wicked ways, then I will hear from heaven, and will forgive their sin and heal their land" **(2 Chron. 7:14).**

Healing starts within each of our hearts. As we walk with Him, we are a light in this world for others, by His grace. Look to the Lord and ask for His help. Repent before the Lord and walk in His promises.

"The humble He guides in justice, / And the humble He teaches His way. / All the paths of the Lord are mercy and truth / To such as keep His covenant and His testimonies. / For Your name's sake, O Lord, / Pardon my iniquity, for it is great" **(Ps. 25:9–11).**

The healing of our land starts within each of our hearts.

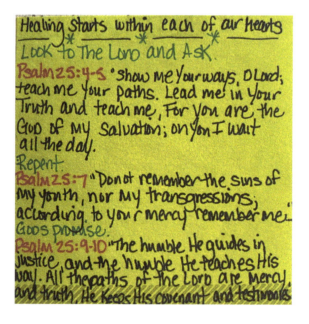

Wake Up! Don't Drift Off to Sleep!

Everything in our lives has been turned upside down due to the COVID pandemic. How we attend church and our workplaces, how children attend school, and even when or how we shop has changed. Everyone across the globe was forced to adopt new ways, some much more extreme than others. A few months after the lockdown in the United States, I saw many (including myself) settling into a new routine and getting used to a new way of life as pandemic conditions continued.

As families became more isolated and the body of Christ met online, the Lord warned my heart, by His Spirit: Don't fall asleep! *Wake up!* In my mind, I pictured a hammock and the body of Christ in it rocking, getting comfortable in these new ways, and slowly drifting off to sleep. I believe it was a warning and a call to us not to get too comfortable or complacent spiritually, to be slowly lulled into a way of life out of fellowship with the body of Christ (and for some, communion with the Lord). It is still relevant today.

Let us join in prayer: *Father, help us to seek You personally and to reach out to others "to stir up the gift of God which is in you through the laying on of hands"* **(2 Tim. 1:6)**. *Help us to encourage one another, Lord, and to press on to the upward calling of Christ Jesus! We have no time to waste.*

Read the context of each scripture in **Romans, 1 Corinthians,** and **Ephesians**.

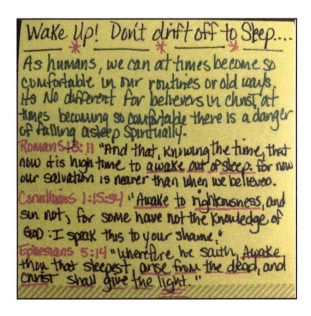

The Importance of Fellowship

Have you ever thought about what the word *fellowship* means to us as believers in Christ? I've noted a few favorite descriptor words pulled up from dictionaries (feel free to look up a few of your own as well):

Fellowship—companionship, togetherness, a community.

Unity—oneness.

We are called to grow closer together (fellowship) in oneness (unity) with the *Lord* and with *each other*.

Read **Hebrews 10:19–25.** It addresses and describes what fellowship with God looks like (vv. 19–22) and what fellowship with one another looks like (vv. 24–25).

We are called to *consider* one another, to *stir up* love and good works in one another, and to *exhort* (or strongly encourage) one another. Seeking fellowship with the Lord first with a pure heart and communing with Him enables us to walk in unity within the community of Christ. This is a beautiful picture of fellowship. Let's not forsake it today.

May the Lord use us instead to sharpen one another **(***See* **Prov. 27:17).**

Talk to the Lord about communing with Him, be in unity with Him, and let His love flow through your fellowship within the body of Christ.

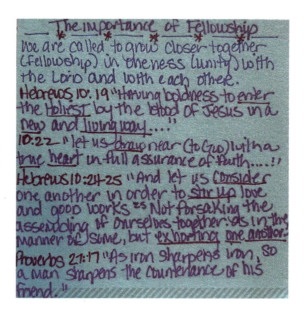

A Daily Walk

The Lord is ready to meet with us each day. He is ready to commune with us and invest in our relationship with Him.

Picture a little table with two chairs—one chair for Him and one chair for you. He never leaves this table; He is always ready to visit with you. Sometimes, you may feel like you're alone, in a spiritual wilderness or desert, or living through a trial too difficult to bear. Maybe you're in the midst of a wonderful time of growth with Him. No matter your circumstance, He is there waiting to fellowship and commune with you to help you through *this* day. Focus on *today*.

Let us examine our personal walk with the Lord. Let Him show you where help is needed drawing close to Him. May we "live and move and have our being" **(Acts 17:28)** in Him each day.

He is ready to help you today, and in His faithfulness, He will be waiting and watching for you, ready to help you through this day and again tomorrow.

Focus on and seek Him today. Read the context of each scripture and talk to Him about your three personal questions.

> **A Daily Walk — Focus on Today**
>
> FOCUS ON TODAY.
> Matthew 6:33-34 "But seek ye first the Kingdom of God and His righteousness, and all these things shall be added to you. Therefore do not worry about tomorrow, for tomorrow will worry about its own things. Sufficient for the day is its own trouble."
>
> In Him we live, and move, and have our being.
> Acts 17:27-28 "That they should seek the Lord, and perhaps feel their way toward Him and find Him. Yet He is actually not far from each one of us, for, 'In Him we live and move and have our being.'"
>
> The Lord is ready to help you today, and will be ready again tomorrow.
>
> Psalm 14:2 "The Lord looked down from heaven upon the children of men, to see if there were any that did understand, and SEEK GOD."

Rest in the Lord

In *every* circumstance, the Lord wants us to *rest* in Him. As we draw close to Him each day to commune and fellowship with Him, we can receive His rest.

How? What does this look like? He gives us instructions and promises in **Matthew 11**:

- Come to Him—fellowship with Him daily.
- Take His yoke—take His guidance and do things His way.
- Learn from Him—listen, heed His Word, and obey.

The Lord uses symbolism and parables to help us understand. In this case, He uses an example of a yoke. I totally get that this is likely not something we see every day; however, the picture is still perfectly relevant. This was a tool used regularly by people when Jesus walked the earth. A yoke is a wooden beam normally used between a pair of oxen or other animals to enable them to *pull together* on a load when working in pairs (go ahead, look up a picture online). It is used to steer, guide, and share the load.

All this to get the job done.

The Lord will bear our burdens completely if we let Him. His yoke, His way, is easy, and His burden is light. He gives rest to our souls, even if our outward circumstances have not changed in a way we physically see. Choose to rest in Him today.

Read and take time to understand the context in which our scripture in **Matthew 11** was written. Talk to Him about your three personal questions.

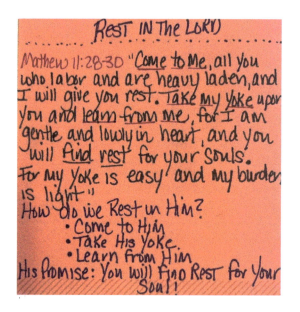

Be Separate

When we believe in Christ, the Holy Spirit takes up residence within us. God's *great power* lives within us. He changes and transforms our hearts, desires, and actions.

As the Master Potter, He molds and shapes us and does His good work in and through us.

When we look back, we realize we are different! Thank you, Lord! It makes us different within the world we live in. Do not be afraid to be separate for Christ. Do not be afraid to be non-conforming to the ways of this world.

Choose in your heart to be set apart. The Lord, by His Spirit, will help you do the rest. He made us and calls us to this purpose.

"'Therefore, come out from among them and be separate,' says the Lord. 'Do not touch what is unclean, and I will receive you'" **(2 Cor. 6:17)**.

Read the context of the scripture provided and talk to Him about your three personal questions. How are you set apart and separate for Him today? How does He want to help you?

> **Be Separate**
>
> 2 Cor. 6:17 "Therefore go out from their midst, and be separate from them," says the Lord, "and touch no unclean thing."
>
> Don't be afraid to *be separate* for Christ and *non-conforming* to the ways of this world.
>
> Romans 12:2 "Do not conform to the patterns of this world, but be transformed by the renewing of your mind. Then you will be able to test and approve what God's will is — his good, pleasing and perfect will."

Walk His Way

The Lord *delights* in us when we walk in His way. He delights in us so much that even when we stumble on this walk, the Lord upholds us with His hand. He *holds* us and *helps* us!

"The steps of a good man are ordered by the Lord, / And He delights in his way, / Though he fall, he shall not be utterly cast down; / For the Lord upholds *him with His hand.*" **(Ps. 37:23–24)**

Our heavenly Father orders our steps! Do you have a desire to walk in them? I do! I so want the Lord to be delighted in my obedience in the walk He ordered for me. In my own strength, I will fail.

How can we do this? **Psalm 37** gives us instruction and hope:

- Do not worry or fret (v. 1).
- Trust in the Lord (v. 3).
- Commit your way to the Lord (v. 5).
- Rest in the Lord and wait patiently for Him (v. 7).

Friends, we can only do this by His Spirit. Let us live **Galatians 5:25 NIV** and "Keep in step with the Spirit!"

Everything and always for His glory, Amen. Talk with Him.

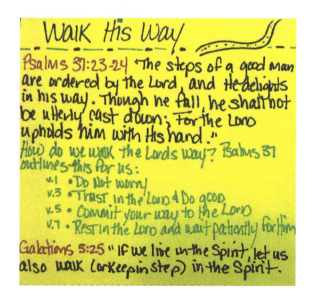

Enjoy His Journey for You

Do you believe the Lord has a journey just for you?

Jeremiah 29:11 NKJV says, "'For I know the thoughts I think toward you,' says the Lord, 'thoughts of peace and not of evil, to give you a future and a hope.'"

When you read the context of why and when the Lord said this, you will see He was talking to His beloved people whom He *allowed* to be taken into captivity under the reign of Nebuchadnezzar of Babylon. Yep. He allowed His people to go through a time of exile for their good! Their hearts had turned away from Him, yet He made a way for them to have peace, a future, and a hope, even through the difficult circumstance of exile. Keep in mind, if they had walked *His* way with Him, the journey may not have led them to exile!

Nonetheless, our Lord wants to take us on His adventure. Jump in and enjoy your journey with Him! Seek Him, listen, respond obediently, and walk each day resting in Him. In this, we can rejoice! Our Father is about His business, and He wants us to jump, by His Spirit, into what He is already doing for His glory! How wonderful it is when He gives us eyes to see His good work!

Rejoice! Be rooted and built up in Him! With thanksgiving, trust that He will complete the good work He started in you *through* His journey for you.

Read through the context of each scripture and talk to Him.

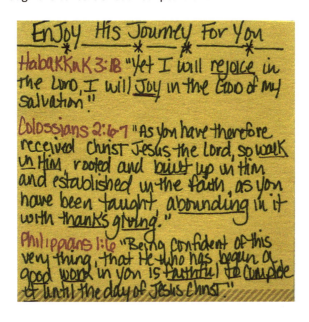

Build Your House on the Rock

> Having been built on the foundation of the apostles and prophets, Jesus Christ Himself being the chief cornerstone, in whom the whole building, being fitted together, grows into a holy temple in the Lord, in whom you also are being built together for a dwelling place of God in the Spirit. **(Ephesians 2:20–22)**

The picture given in this scripture is wonderful. Jesus Christ is the Chief Cornerstone. He is the main foundational rock that all others are built upon. He bears the weight and holds it all in place, which is the first step to building a solid foundation. Maybe you are not too familiar with construction work. In the States, we typically don't build foundations out of individual stones anymore. Go ahead and look up examples of cornerstones online. Look at pictures. Pull out a dictionary and get a good visual in mind.

We, likewise, are a dwelling place, a house for and of God by His Holy Spirit. Our heavenly Father is in control of our lives; He builds them and builds us up with Jesus Christ as the chief cornerstone of our lives of faith.

Read **Matthew 7:24–27**. It further reminds us that if we build our house upon the rock, it will stand, no matter the storm that comes. But if any man builds his house on sand, it will fall, and it will be a great fall. We have nothing to fear if we let the Lord build our houses, our lives, upon the saving grace of Jesus Christ.

"Unless the Lord builds the house, / They labor in vain who build it" **(Ps. 127:1)**.

The Lord instructs us to take care with building our houses (the building of our lives

Let's not waste time doing things our own way; our job is to believe in Jesus Christ, the Chief Cornerstone, and stand firmly on the rock! Our heavenly Father does the building in His time as we follow Him. By His grace and strength, we will be able to stand and weather every storm.

> **Build Your House on The Rock**
>
> Matthew 7:24-27 "Therefore whoever hears these sayings of Mine, and does them, I will liken Him to a wise man who built his house on the rock: and the rain descended, the floods came, and the winds blew and beat on that house; and it did not fall, for it was founded on the rock. But everyone who hears these sayings of mine, and does not do them will be like a foolish man who built his house on the sand: and the rains descended, the floods came, and the winds blew and beat on that house; and it fell. And it was a great fall."
>
> Do Not Fear. LET The LORD Build Your House!

Pray the Lord Sends Laborers into His Harvest

We cannot deny that our world is in a state of uncertainty and chaos; sin abounds as so many are blind to the truth. My hope is in the Lord, and I hold fast to it!

I'm reminded of **Matthew 9:36–38** and the example and instruction Jesus gave. Jesus saw that many were weary and scattered with no shepherd, and He had compassion. He said to pray to the Lord of the harvest to send His laborers into His harvest. Isn't that prayer so applicable to us today? So needed?

Will you join me in praying for these things:

- Ask to have the compassion of Jesus, by His Spirit, for others in this world.
- Ask to be led by Jesus to plant, sow, and water, according to His will.
- Ask for the Lord of the harvest to send out laborers into His harvest.
- Ask for repentance, revival, and God's mercy in our nation for His people and the world.

I thank our heavenly Father for stirring up a desire in our hearts to pray in compassion. This is a desire that is supernatural and comes by His Holy Spirit to those who believe and are willing vessels. He will use us as His hands and feet on this earth, as His fellow laborers in the harvest.

Read the scripture in context in **Matthew**. Please join me in prayer and talk to our heavenly Father about your three personal questions and His will for your hands and feet.

We Are Laborers Together with God

Our last devotional message focused on the Lord's direction in **Matthew 9:36–38**. He said, "Pray the Lord of the *Harvest* to send His laborers *into His Harvest*" (emphasis added).
Do you believe that is you, that you are the one He sends?

First Corinthians 3:9 KJV says, "For we are laborers together with God."

We are His hands and feet! We can only do this by His Spirit! We reap what we sow, both in our own lives and as we walk in love toward others. You see, as we walk with the Lord each day, believing in Him, asking Him to use us as His willing vessels, He will orchestrate the perfect opportunities to sow, plant, or water the for the Kingdom of God: He will bring someone in the body of Christ to you whom He may give you a kind word for. He may allow you to cross paths with another person and sharpen each other by His Spirit. And He can orchestrate the path of an unbeliever so that you can present the gospel message to them. Our job is to believe, be willing, be ready, and be obedient to the Holy Spirit's prompting; our faithful God does the rest!

Read the scriptures in context and talk to Him about your three personal questions.

Let us pray: *Lord, help us to believe that You equip us as Your laborers. Help us to walk according to Your will to plant, sow, and water. Bring the harvest, Lord, and raise up Your laborers into Your harvest.*

God Brings the Harvest

Thank you, Lord, that You equip us to be your hands and feet!

When we pray for His way, we may never know how God may architect and orchestrate our lives for His divine purpose. I can remember a time, in stepping out in faith to stand and lead a Christian life group within the workplace, when I asked the Lord to raise up and bring leaders within the workplace who loved Him and had true hearts. In another specific prayer, I asked God to bring forward another lady to help teach a women's Bible study in our local office. God brought forward a precious woman who loves the Lord, has a gift for loving others to the max, and she said to me, "Darlene, I just want to have a Bible study that teaches right out of the Bible!" The Lord immediately spoke to me and said, "She is your co-teacher." To this day, years later, she is still one of my closest friends (she knows who she is!).

Sometimes, I may not fully understand a divine crossroad He orchestrates. What may seem like a brief moment of sharing God's Word, an encouragement, a confirmation, or the gospel message, the Lord orchestrates for His glory according to His master plan! He knows how to connect us for His glory, and He knows how to draw us unto Himself.

Our Savior, our Lord, *is* the Lord of the harvest.

We may be called in moments to plant, sow, or water, but it is always God who brings the increase. He is the one who connects us for His purpose and turns hearts unto salvation for eternal life. He is the one who gathers us unto Himself in heaven!

> God Brings The Harvest!
>
> We are Gods labourers, His hands and feet on this earth! Glory to Him.
>
> 1 Cor 3:6-9 (Paul said) "I planted, Apollos watered, but God gave the increase. So then neither he who plants is anything, nor he who waters, but God who gives the increase. ⁸ Now he who plants and he who waters are one, and each one will receive his own reward according to his own labor. ⁹ For we are God's fellow workers; you are God's field, you are God's building."
>
> Luke 17:5 "And the apostles said to the Lord, 'Increase our faith.'"

Go! The Time Is Now

There is such an urgency in my heart to encourage fellow believers in Christ that we are the ones God sends into His harvest **(1 Cor. 3:9)**! What a call to action we have to be His laborers *and* to also pray He sends us out **(Matt. 9:36–38)**.

As God calls on you, *Go!* The time is *now*.

Sometimes, I think we create a picture in our minds of what we think this has to look like. Maybe it's a thought that you have to be accomplished in certain areas of your life, a good speaker, a seminary graduate, called to the mission field in some far-off place. These things are not bad, and some are called to them, but God wants to use us in our ordinary, everyday, walk-with-Him lives! I have to admit, there have been instances that I have felt less than, not good enough, or not worthy to do something in the name of the Lord when I felt His prompting. I have met others whose intent to move in love was paralyzed by the notion they felt like they were not worthy enough.

Well, in our own strength, we are unable to answer God's call. Sometimes, the lies of the enemy or the words or actions of others towards us may have created wounds that cause us to believe we are less than. However, at some point we have to *believe* that God is within us. We have to believe we are of value to Him. We have to believe in His equipping and we have to be willing to step forward in what He has for us according to His plan.

Let's not discount who God is *within* us. There is no boundary with our God in how He can use your life! *He can connect you with others for His divine purpose anywhere and anytime He desires to.* Be ready to give a testament of His goodness or to share His good news as He leads.

Let us pray: *Lord, help us to believe that You equip us as Your laborers. Help us to walk according to Your will to plant, sow, and water. Bring the harvest, Lord, and raise up Your laborers for Your harvest!*

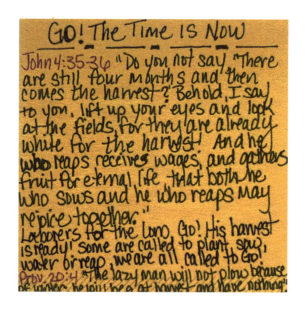

Hope

I am so thankful for the *hope* we have through Christ Jesus during the short time we are on this earth.

In the midst of the chaos of this world we live in, I'm reminded of **Psalm 24:1–2 NKJV:** "The earth is the Lord's, and all its fullness, / The world and those who dwell therein. / For He has founded it upon the seas, / And established it upon the waters."

God is sovereign over this world and our life on earth, and through Jesus, we have a Savior, salvation, and eternal life! Lord, help us have *hope* in Your glory! Help us to receive and walk in Your love.

If you look up the word *hope* in a current dictionary, you will see descriptions like these: to *desire* with expectation, to *expect* with confidence.

Personally, I'm asking the Lord to help me walk each day with this perspective of hope:

Heavenly

Outlook with

Purpose and

Expectation

Help us, Lord, to do this as we receive Your love.

My prayer is for fresh hope and fresh faith to be stirred in your heart and spirit. Talk to our heavenly Father about your three personal questions. What might He want to say to you?

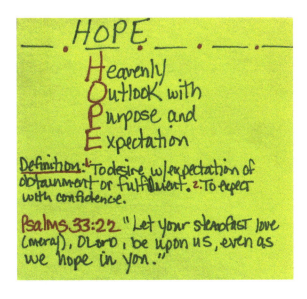

For His Glory | 129

Our Hope Is in the Lord

Our *hope* is in the Lord! We are made to desire to know our heavenly Father more and more. We are created to rest in Him. We can expect and trust with confidence that He meets all physical and spiritual needs: sometimes, in ways we could never imagine; sometimes, in ways we would not expect; and sometimes, He does His work in the waiting. Walking with our eyes on the Lord means to walk each day with the Holy Spirit's help and with **H O P E**—a **H**eavenly **O**utlook with **P**urpose and **E**xpectation.

We can walk in confidence as we hope in the Lord. I don't mean arrogant or prideful confidence, but confidence that is bold and resolved to rest in Him, regardless of what things may look like. As His Word says, we can hope in the Lord.

Read the scripture provided in **Psalms 33 and 31**:

- He delivers us from death (our souls).
- He keeps us alive in famine.
- He is our help.
- He is our shield (protector).
- His steadfast love is upon us.
- He shall strengthen our hearts.

What proclamations of His promise and love He gives us! Let's choose to let our hearts and souls rest in Him.

Do you need help resting in the daily *HOPE* of who He is? I know I do. It only comes through a relationship with our heavenly Father. Talk with Him about your three personal questions and how He may want to help you grow in this type of *HOPE*.

> Our HOPE is in the LORD!
>
> Psalm 33:18-22 "Behold, the eye of the Lord is upon them that fear him, upon them that hope in his mercy (steadfast love); To deliver their soul from death, and to keep them alive in famine. Our soul waiteth for the Lord: he is our help and our shield. For our heart shall rejoice in him, because we have trusted in his holy name. Let thy mercy (steadfast love), O Lord, be upon us, according as we hope in thee."
>
> Psalm 31:24 "Be of good courage, And He shall strengthen your heart, All you

Persevere in Hope

One way to define the word *persevere* is a *continued* effort to do or achieve something, despite difficulty or opposition.

We have to *choose* to press on, to continue to lay hold of God's promises, and to press forward in Christ. When we persevere by the grace of God, we have *hope* in the midst of our circumstances. We need this message so much today. Many close friends are missing loved ones who are now in heaven. We live in a time of economic and political turmoil when what is good may be called bad, and what is bad may be called good. Oh yeah, and there is still a pandemic in which we are constantly being warned that another strain may come around the corner that could evade our immunity. Our sovereign God sees it all and is in control of it all. Yet 2020 recorded the highest number of deaths due to overdose! So many need *hope* in God.

Isaiah 40:31 gives us a promise: "Those who wait on the Lord will renew their strength."

When we press on, lay hold of God's promises, and reach forward toward the upward calling of Christ, we can walk daily in God's grace (persevere). It's always and only for God's glory!

Let us pray: *God, you gave us Your Son as the light of the world; help us to shine by His grace and all for Your glory, Lord. No matter our circumstance, help us to choose You and to walk in Your promises. You are always faithful, Lord. Help me to be Your light in this time to all around me who may need Your hope. Amen.*

Talk with Him.

> **Persevere in Hope**
> Think about what *persevere* means.
> 1. We have to choose to persevere.
> 2. We can only do this with God's help.
>
> Philippians 3:12-15 gives further instruction:
> - Press on
> - Lay hold
> - Forget what's behind
> - Reach forward
> - Press toward the goal of Christ
> - Walk by this rule
> - Have the same mind
>
> When we continue in a state of grace (persevere) the Lord leads us to a state of His glory. Hold on!
> Isaiah 40:31 Those who hope in the Lord will renew their strength......

Our Hope and Help

I don't know how many times during the pandemic I heard, "I can't wait until this is all over!" Somehow, if life went back to the way it was prior to the pandemic all things would be instantly wonderful. Yet even with the difficulties of 2020 and 2021 behind us and things opening up as our lives return to "normal" busyness, it seems to me that the difficulties we live with are not really better. They may just be a little different, and so many are still losing heart.

I want to testify that I'm thankful for all the circumstances above. It is not easy, but a thankful heart is what brought me hope during the pandemic and today! I'm thankful that the Lord stopped the world for a time so we could all reflect on what is important. I'm thankful for the good that came for many.

Ephesians 5 shares that we should give thanks *always* to God—always—in every circumstance, year, and day.

Do not lose heart!

Therefore we do not lose heart. Even though our outward man is perishing, yet the inward man is being renewed day by day. For our light affliction which is but for a moment, is working for us a far more exceeding and eternal weight of glory, while we do not look at the things which are seen, but at the things which are not seen. The things which are seen are temporary, but the things which are not seen are eternal." **(2 Corinthians 4:16–18)**

In the midst of our temporary affliction, God's promise is to renew us day by day, and by His Spirit, He speaks to us saying, "This *is* the way; walk in it" **(Isa. 30:20–21)**.

Read each scripture and talk to Him about your three personal questions.

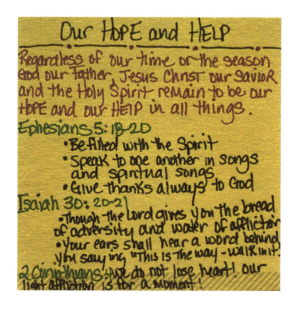

Standing and Suffering for Christ

God is our *hope* and *help* in *all* things. Our circumstances in this world may seem increasingly difficult. Do you ever feel overwhelmed by it? The Word of God gives us direction on how to stand and suffer for Christ. He gives us a call to action and a promise.

In **Philippians 1:27–30**, He calls us:

- To let our conduct be worthy of the gospel of Christ;
- To stand fast in one spirit, with one mind;
- To strive together for the faith of the gospel;
- To believe in Him;
- To suffer for His name's sake.

In the midst of this, God's promises stand:

- The promise of salvation **(Phil. 1:28)**
- The Lord's promise to deliver His righteous ones from all affliction **(Ps. 34:19)**

He wants us to be yielded to His will and way of deliverance, trusting Him even in the storm. God our Father is faithful, and He is sovereign over every circumstance we see and live in today.

Talk to our heavenly Father about your three personal questions. Is there a difficult circumstance in your life that He wants you to walk through? Have you been longsuffering for others? Do you feel oppressed where He has you? Talk to Him about it and let Him talk to you. Our faithful Father has a purpose in everything.

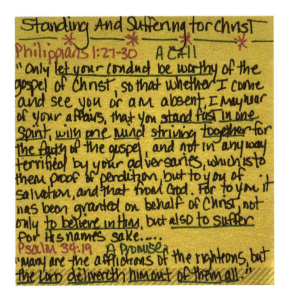

For His Glory | 133

Look Up, Press In, and Press On

The Lord calls us to look to Him each day for all things, in every circumstance.

He calls us to press into Him, building our relationship and trust in Him with grateful hearts. In **Philippians 3**, Paul exhorted us to press on toward the goal of the prize of the upward call of Christ!

What is our upward call? To walk each day as He anoints and appoints each of us for His glory! We are the light of His love in the darkness. But we can only do this by looking up, pressing in, and pressing on! This is a choice. What will you choose today?

Where or how in your life might He need you to choose this response? Talk to Him about your three personal questions.

> LOOK UP! Press IN and Press ON!
> This is a choice. What choice will you make?
> Isaiah 45:22 "Look to me, and be saved, all you ends of the earth! For I am God, and there is no other."
> How do we press IN and Press ON?
> Read Philippians 3:13-21 + 4:1 - Highlights
> v.12 • but I press on that I may lay hold of that which Christ Jesus also laid hold of me.
> v.13 • Forget things behind us.
> • Reach forward to what lies ahead.
> v.14 • Press toward the goal for the prize of the upward call of Christ Jesus.
> • We eagerly wait for our Savior
> v.4:1 • STAND FAST IN THE LORD!

Abound in Hope

As Paul spoke to the believing Romans, he gave this word: "Now may the God of hope fill you with all joy and peace in believing, that you may abound in hope by the power of the Holy Spirit" **(Rom. 15:13)**.

As I read the context of why he said this, I see it as a word of encouragement and direction and a blessing over the body of Christ all at the same time!

This is my heart in Christ for you. Read the context of scripture in **Romans 15** and **Hebrews 11:1–2**.

Walk in His joy, peace, and rest each day. It is only by His Spirit we can do this, especially in a troubled, sin-sick world. Do you see how setting your heart on this sets you apart in this world? This is active faith. Even though the world today may not see Jesus in His flesh, the world will see Jesus in and through you!

This is a testament that makes us His witnesses of "things not seen." Be blessed abundantly, and may you abound in hope by the power of the Holy Spirit.
Talk with Him.

> **Abound in Hope**
> We can both rest and rejoice in hope in God because He gave us Christ Jesus. Romans 15:13 "Now may the God of hope fill you with all joy and peace in believing, that you may abound in hope by the power of the Holy Spirit."
> As we Hope by the Power of the Holy Spirit in things unseen, this is our Faith in Action! As witnesses with a changed life, we are evidence now seen.
> Hebrews 11:1 "Now Faith is the substance of things hoped for, the evidence of things not seen."

God Keeps Our Peace

Do you believe that when you look to the Lord and trust in Him, He can keep your heart and mind in perfect peace, no matter the circumstance?

He can, but it requires us to make a choice:

- We have to choose *to look to* Him.
- We have to choose *to take thoughts captive by* His power.
- We have to choose *to rest in* His peace.

In **Mark 4:39**, Jesus and His disciples were in a boat when a storm came upon them. The disciples were overcome with fear. Jesus said, "'Peace, be still!' and the wind ceased, and there was a great calm."

In this same way, we can take thoughts captive with God's power by His Spirit living in us!

Sometimes, we have to choose to say, "Anger, you have no place in my heart! Fear, get behind me! Satan, you have no dominion to hurt my mind with thoughts!" As we take thoughts captive and look to Him, He will keep us in perfect peace.

Read the context of the scriptures provided in **Isaiah, 2 Corinthians,** and **Mark**. Talk to Him about your three personal questions and how He wants to help you in this area.

> **God Keeps Our Peace**
>
> Isaiah 26:3 "You will keep him in perfect peace, whose mind is stayed on You, because he trusts in You."
>
> Do you believe when you look to the Lord, when you trust Him, He will give your heart and mind peace? Sometimes, we have to fight to focus our heart & mind on Him. We have to choose to take captive our thoughts.
>
> 2 Corinthians 10:5 "We take captive every thought to make it obedient to Christ."
>
> In the midst of a storm Jesus rebuked the wind and invited calm. That same power lives in You!
>
> Mark 4:39 "Then He arose and rebuked the wind and said to the sea, 'PEACE, BE STILL'!"

Give Thanks and Live Wisely

This particular devotional was written in February of 2021.

What a week we just had in Texas! We had unconventional sub-freezing weather, no electricity or water, a shortage of gasoline, and most public locations were closed. I am so thankful for all the little things that are actually big. I've never been so thankful for the huge pile of firewood my husband keeps ready (that I had always thought was a bit excessive) for his delicious Texas barbeque; this week, it was fuel for the fire that cooked our food, kept us warm, and supplied the neighbors.

It moves my heart to a place of compassion for so many in our world who live without basic comforts and privileges every day: it could be freedom, a roof, or necessities like water, food, clothing, or medical care. Let's stop today and thank Him; we are all so privileged in our country compared to so many others, and I know I have, at times, taken it for granted.

I'm so grateful for our Lord and His mercy over us!

Read **Psalm 103**. Bless the Lord! Praise Him for all His benefits! He knows our frailty and every need. With not a cent to our names, we can have everything in Him. His mercy is forever!

Our lives are so short!

"As for a man, his days are like grass; / As a flower in a field, so he flourishes. / For the wind passes over and it is gone" **(Ps. 103:15–16).**

Ephesians 5:15–16 NIV says, "Look carefully then how you live, not as unwise but as wise, making the most of every opportunity, because the days are evil."

May we each gratefully and thankfully make the most of each day that He gifts to us, for His glory.

Read each scripture in context. Talk to Him about your three questions. Thank Him for all.

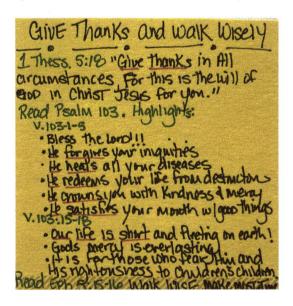

Be Reconciled to God

It's the morning of a most holy day starting a most holy week. This week marks days of Passover: Palm Sunday, Good Friday, and Resurrection Sunday. Several biblical and historical events all happened in this weekly timeframe at different years in history: About 1446 BC marks the time God delivered Israel from bondage in Egypt; it is the time God made a way for His people to be spared from the passing "death angel" by the blood of a pure and spotless lamb on the door posts. It marks the time Israel started to wander in the wilderness. In AD 30, this week marks the time of Jesus's crucifixion, death, and resurrection.

Think about the significance of this timeframe and each of these events and what the outcome means to us today!

Read **Romans 5:6–11.**

"For if we were enemies we were reconciled to God through the death of His Son, much more, having been reconciled, we shall be saved by His Life" **(Rom. 5:10 NKJV).**

Think about what the word *reconcile* really means. The definition of the root word in Greek (*katallass'o*) means: to *decisively* change, exchange, and come together to the same position.

Friends, we were once enemies of God. However, He made a way through Jesus Christ for us to *decide to change*, to *exchange* our fleshly nature for His way, and to *come together and stand with Christ*. We are no longer enemies but friends of God.

That is the fullness of being reconciled to Him! Let's rejoice in the goodness of who He is for us and the fact that, through reconciliation, we are saved and free!

Talk to Him.

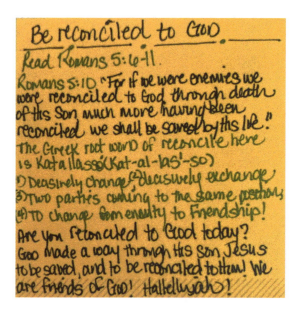

God Equips You as He Calls You

Do you believe God equips you and anoints you for what He calls you to do?

Second Corinthians 12:9 says, "And He said to me, 'My grace is sufficient for you, for My strength is made perfect in weakness.'"

As you obediently walk in what He calls you to do, fully leaning on His strength, He will equip you with everything you need!

Let's look at the story of Daniel, a wonderful example of God's equipping and anointing in weakness and obedience. There is no task too big or too small for God's equipping and anointing. When it is His will, it is important to Him!

Read **Daniel chapters 1 and 2**. When Daniel and his three companions interacted with King Nebuchadnezzar, God equipped them with favor, knowledge, skill, wisdom, and understanding.

Why? Because Daniel asked for God's mercy and help in obedience to what he was called to. Without God's help, they faced death.

God equips us in our weakness for His glory and according to His will. Ask Him to help you believe and to walk in it.

Read all scripture provided in context and talk with Him about your three personal questions.

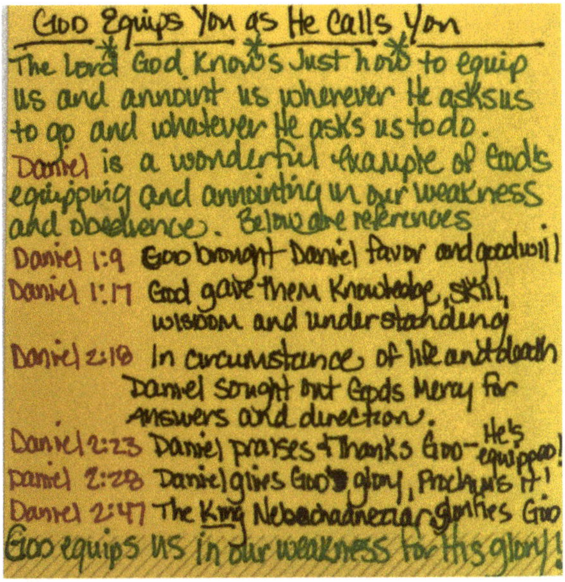

Handwritten note:

God Equips You as He Calls You

The Lord God knows just how to equip us and anoint us wherever He asks us to go and whatever He asks us to do.

Daniel is a wonderful example of God's equipping and anointing in our weakness and obedience. Below are references.

Daniel 1:9 — God brought Daniel favor and goodwill

Daniel 1:17 — God gave them knowledge, skill, wisdom and understanding

Daniel 2:18 — In circumstance of life and death Daniel sought out God's mercy for answers and direction.

Daniel 2:23 — Daniel praises & thanks God — He's equipped!

Daniel 2:28 — Daniel gives God's glory, Proclaims it!

Daniel 2:47 — The King Nebuchadnezzar glorifies God

God equips us in our weakness for His glory!

Rend Your Heart Unto the Lord

"Even now," declares the Lord, "return to me with all your heart, with fasting and weeping and mourning." Rend your heart and not your garments. Return to the Lord your God, for he is gracious and compassionate, slow to anger and abounding in love, and he relents from sending calamity. **(Joel 2:13 ESV)**

What does "rend your heart" mean? I realize that in today's day and age, we don't use the word *rend* too much on a day-to-day basis. Nonetheless, the meaning of it in the context of the book of Joel is so powerful and life-giving.

The meaning of the Hebrew root word is "to tear." It was customary in Jewish expression to tear garments and put on sackcloth and ashes when mourning the death of a relative.

To "rend your heart and not your garments" means it's not about an outward appearance of mourning or repentance; it's about an inward working and baring of the heart before our Lord—a true heart's cry, repentant and baring all, and an inward dying to self for the glory of God. Lord, have Your way in us!

Read the scripture in Joel in context and talk to our Lord about your three personal questions.

God Will Speak to You—Listen

We read in God's Word of all these miraculous ways God spoke to His people: Moses and the burning bush, angels visibly appearing to give word or direction, and the pillar of fire that led the Israelites through the wilderness, to name just a few. Can God still speak to us in these ways? Of course, He can! He is God, and He has no boundaries.

With that said, we don't normally hear of Him speaking to us in the ways listed above. But the voice of God is *real*. He speaks, and He is ready to speak to you!

It requires us to stop, enter into His presence, and listen. We can't hear Him in our self-sufficiency or if our eyes and ears are not open as we walk and commune with Him. There is no boundary for God and His Spirit in how He can speak to you. I could never list all the ways He speaks, but He is the still, small voice in the quiet; the internal, loud voice that can stop you in your tracks; the burning of the heart and soul as you commune with Him; the dreams and visions of revelation, through His Word and His creation; and He can deliver a word through another in the body of Christ.

Friends, He speaks! Read the scripture provided in context in the **Psalms** and **John.** Talk with Him about your three questions. Wait on Him and listen.

> God Will Speak To You – Listen!
>
> Psalm 85:8 "I will hear what God the LORD will speak, For He will speak peace To His people and to His saints; But let them not turn back to folly."
>
> The voice of God is real. He speaks and He is ready to speak to You! However, it requires us to STOP, enter into His presence and LISTEN! Anything else is folly!
>
> John 10:27 "My sheep hear My voice, and I know them, and they follow Me."
>
> As believers in Christ, we are His sheep & He is our great shepherd. When we listen, we know the voice of our Shepherd!

Ever Asked God "Why?"

Have you ever been in the midst of a life circumstance when you have just asked God "Why?" *Why is this hard? God? Why don't you _____? Why didn't you _____? Why is this happening?*

We face difficulty when someone we know and love is experiencing the consequences of sin (disobedient action), and our lives are impacted by it. Our nation, our world as a whole, is disobedient to God, living in sin, calling sin good and good things evil. I'm not talking about asking God "Why?" in these circumstances. However, for the righteous child of God who trusts and is obedient to the Lord and knows God is in control, have you ever been tempted to ask God "Why?"

Habakkuk was in this place; he asked God why He was tolerating wrongdoing and even accused God of not listening! In **Habakkuk 1:5 NIV**, God responded to Him: "Look among the Nations and watch—and be utterly amazed. For I am going to do something in your days that you would not believe, even if you were told." Amazing!

Our God is sovereign over *all* things! He is always working things for the good of those who love Him, even when He allows difficult circumstances.

For me, God has taught me through His faithfulness. He has taught me through a cancer diagnosis, seven surgeries, and eighteen months of chemo. He's taught me through not being able to have my own biological children. He's taught me through persecution, oppression in the workplace, and rejection even from loved ones.

Through it all, He's changed my heart's cry from asking "Why?" to instead asking *"What, would you have me do, Lord, according to Your plan and for Your glory?"* I believe in who You are, God.

He is always faithful. Choose to praise Him and thank Him, even in the storm. Even Habakkuk had a heart turned to praise; check out chapter 3.

Read the scripture in context and talk to God about your three personal questions.

Walk by Faith

"For we walk by faith, not by sight" **(2 Cor. 5:7 NKJV)**.

Who knew that one line of scripture, eight words, could have such an impact?

It seems simple, yet it is powerful. It is a statement, yet it is also direction for us. It is direction that highlights *what* to do in the life of a Christian and *how* to do it.

So, what does *walk* mean in this scripture? Well, literally, the Greek root word means, "to walk" and its usage means "I conduct my life, live." Another way to think of this scripture's meaning is that *we conduct our lives, or live, by faith and not by sight*.

To "walk by faith" means to walk with God. Let me repeat that: walk *with* God. Let's think of a picture to help us. Imagine walking arm in arm, side by side, and step-by-step with God each day. That means we are not walking in front of God or several steps behind Him. It certainly means we don't turn around and walk away from Him.

How can we walk *with* Him?

- We can walk *with* God because of Christ **(2 Cor. 3:4–6)**.
- We can walk *with* God if we are rooted and built up in Him. It is a daily walk **(Col. 2:6–7)**.
- We can walk *with* God by having a pure and clean heart before God **(James 4:8)**.

How are we instructed to walk *with* Him?

- Walk by the Spirit—free **(2 Cor. 3:17–18)**.
- Keep in step with the Spirit **(Gal. 5:25)**.
- Walk in wisdom **(Eph. 5:15–16)**.
- Walk humbly **(Mic. 6:8)**.

Walking by faith *with* God can be done by having a full relationship with Him. It requires action on our part and a choice to ask for His help to do all things each day. He is faithful!

Take your time talking and communing with the Lord regarding your three personal questions. Read each scripture and ensure that you understand its context.

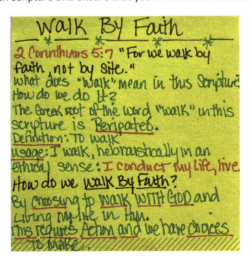

Not by Sight

In our previous devotional, we were reminded of the importance of walking *with* God and what that means. Let's focus now on the word *faith*.

Hebrews 11:1 defines *faith* in a wonderful way: "Now Faith is the substance of things hoped for, the evidence of things not seen."

Do you *believe* that Christ Jesus working *in* and *through* you is evidence of things not seen?

How often are your actions influenced by what you physically see? How often are others influenced by your actions? Have you ever heard someone say something like, "I'll believe it when I see it"?

When it comes to walking *with* God, step-by-step and according to His plan, we can only do it when we choose to ask Him for His help. Our sufficiency is from God **(2 Cor. 3:4–5)**. It is an action of *walking by faith*, living in the moment, even when we do not see what is before us and even when we don't understand what we see. We know we are walking by faith and not by sight when we have *peace* in our hearts as we walk with Him according to His plan, even when we don't know what our next steps may be.

Let us pray: *Lord, help us each to walk with You in Your strength. Amen.*

Talk with Him.

> Walk by FAITH, Not by SITE
> 2 Corinthians 5:7 "For we walk by FAITH, not by SITE".
> What is FAITH? Hebrews 11:1 "Now FAITH is the substance of things hoped for, the EVIDENCE OF THINGS NOT SEEN!"
> Do you believe Christ seen IN AND Through you is that evidence? We can do this by walking with God and asking for His help by the power of His Spirit.
> 2 Corinthians 3:4-5 "And we have such trust through Christ toward God. ⁵ Not that we are sufficient of ourselves, but our sufficiency is from God...".

The Lord Weighs the Heart

The Lord *always* knows, sees, and understands our thoughts, our intentions, and the very motives of our hearts. *Always.* Why do we do the things we do and say the things we say? Our Father sees and knows.

Proverbs 21:2 and **16:2** both reference that every man (mankind) is "right" or pure in his own eyes. Is it true that we may think our hearts are right and pure even when they are not? Yes!

Why is this? I believe it is because of sin in the world and pride in the hearts of mankind. How can we ensure our hearts are right and pure before God? Ask Him to search your heart and expose what is not right and repent before our Father. Let *everything* you do or say come from a heart that wants the pure will of God. You will be able to walk freely with Him and with a peaceful heart.

Ask Him for the desire to want to hear Him say to you, "Well done, good and faithful servant!"

Talk with Him.

True Freedom

Freedom is not defined by where we live, the government we are under, or the man-made laws under which we reside.

True *freedom* is of the heart, the mind, and the soul through Christ Jesus! It has no boundaries and is everlasting! It brings joy overflowing and frees every burden of sin! It is an everlasting promise from God. As we walk in the true freedom of Christ, we become beacons of hope as we trust in Him.

Let's pray: *Lord, we trust You to provide all we need to walk freely in You.*

Read the scripture provided in **John** and **Romans**, take the time to understand the context, and talk with Him about your three personal questions.

> **True Freedom**
>
> John 8: 31-32, 34 "Then Jesus said to those Jews who believed Him, "If you abide in My word, you are My disciples indeed. ³² And you shall know the truth, and the truth shall make you free."
> ³⁴ "Therefore if the Son makes you free, you shall be free indeed."
> True FREEDOM is one of the heart, the mind and the soul through Christ.
> Romans 15:13 "Now may the God of hope fill you with all joy and peace in believing, that you may abound in hope by the power of the Holy Spirit."

Obedience Brings Blessing

The Lord calls us to look to Him, listen for His voice, heed His instruction, and be obedient. Walking each day according to His will also bring His blessing.

Read **Deuteronomy 28:**

Now it shall come to pass, if you diligently obey the voice of the Lord your God, to observe carefully all His commandments which I command you today, that the Lord your God will set you high above the nations of the earth. And all these blessings shall come upon you and overtake you, because you obey the voice of the Lord your God. (**Deuteronomy 28:1–2**)

The remainder of this chapter lists examples of these blessings. However, it also lists the consequences of disobedience. Think about it: Saul, in his disobedience, was removed from being king over Israel. Moses, because of disobedience, was not able to go to the promised land; He only saw it from afar. Jonah, in his disobedience, was swallowed by a whale! Israel was allowed to be in bondage due to their disobedience multiple times. In all these consequences, God's love for each of them never changed.

Let's pray: *Oh Lord, give us a desire to be obedient to* You. *We thank You for Your love, blessing, and correction that is always for our good!*

Read each scripture in context and talk with Him about your three personal questions.

God Can Give One Step at a Time

I love the story of Noah in **Genesis chapters 6–9**. Noah was counted as righteous before the Lord in his time, and God spoke to him. We know the story of how Noah built the ark, but have you ever noticed that God only gave him instruction as he needed it and at the right times?

- "Make yourself an ark of gopherwood" **(Gen. 6:14)**.
- "And every living thing you shall bring two of every sort into the ark" **(Gen. 6:19)**.
- "Then the Lord said to Noah, 'Come into the ark'" **(Gen. 7:1)**.
- "Then God spoke to Noah, saying 'Go out of the ark'" **(Gen. 8:15)**.
- "God blessed Noah and his sons and said, 'Be fruitful and multiply, and fill the earth'" **(Gen. 9:1)**.

All along the way, God gave Noah specific instructions. Do you believe God can do that for you? We need His voice and instruction in all things!

Regardless of our circumstances, we are safe in His presence and hearing His voice. Wait on the Lord.

Read about Noah in **Genesis 6–9** with a new perspective. Read about Samuel in **1 Samuel 16** as he gives step-by-step instructions in who would be anointed king according to God's will.

> God can give ONE STEP AT A TIME
>
> Our faithful Father gives the right amount of instruction at the right time to those who ask, seek and believe.
>
> Reference the story of Noah in Genesis chapters 6-9. God gives Noah several instructions, but not all at once. It was a little at a time and at the right time.
>
> God can give specific instructions like in the example with Samuel after Saul was rejected by God as King of Israel.
>
> 1 Samuel 16:2-3 "And Samuel said, 'How can I go? If Saul hears it, he will kill me.' But the Lord said, 'Take a heifer with you and say, I have come to sacrifice to the Lord.' Then invite Jesse to the sacrifice, and I will show you what to do; you shall anoint for Me the one I name to you.'"

You Are Needed in the Body of Christ

God's plan is so much greater, so much higher than we can imagine. He orchestrates His master plan for our world, yet He knows every need and every desire of our hearts!

Our heavenly Father places each of us, each member of His holy body, just as He pleases and plans. Think about that: your life, your past, the moment you surrendered your heart and gave it to Him leading up to this very moment in time—He has made you and placed you according to His plan! *You are needed, all* who believe in Him are needed, to move and work together as His body to share the gospel message. We are each to plant, water, or sow for the sake of salvation through Jesus Christ according to His will. He has made you for this!

Believe Him. Believe who He made you to be in Him, and believe who He is within you!

Read His Word in **1 Corinthians 12** as indicated below and talk to Him.

> **You ARE NEEDED in The Body of CHRIST**
>
> 1 Corinthians 12:12, 18
> "For as the body is *one* and has many members, but all the members of that one body, being many, are one body, so also *in Christ*."
> v.18 "But now God has set the members, each one of them, in the body just as He pleased."
> We are unified through Christ by one Spirit in the body of Christ. At the same time, God made each member of the body of Christ unique and according to His will. All are needed. You are needed

For His Glory

We Are Called to Share the Gospel Message

Jesus calls us and instructs us to take action in sharing the gospel message.

What is the gospel message? The Greek translation of the noun *gospel* is *euangelion*, literally meaning "good news." The first four books in the New Testament—Matthew, Mark, Luke, and John—are called the Gospels. And the heart of the message in each of them is Christ Jesus: His birth, His life, His death, and His resurrection from the grave for the sake of the gift of salvation available to all. We can see the beautiful simplicity of the gospel message!

Read the scripture in **Matthew 28** in context with the chapter. His instruction is for us all. Be encouraged that as you walk each day according to where He has placed you, He will open the doors and orchestrate those wonderful opportunities to share and testify of who He is by His Spirit. Believe that He always equips you as He calls.

Let's pray: *Lord, help us with the understanding of Your Word. Help us, by Your Spirit, to be sensitive to Your voice when You prompt us to tell others about You. Help us to plant, sow, and water as You call. Lord, bring the harvest! Amen.*

Commissioned for His Mission

We are *all* made for His purpose—all of us—we have to *choose* to walk in it. We have to *choose* to say "Yes" to God, be separate from this world, and to be humbly reconciled to our God with clean hearts.

Lord, help us be obedient! We have been commissioned for His mission! Another way to say this is that *we have each been given instruction and a command to do His important assignment!*

Matthew 28:19 instructs us to "Go therefore and make disciples of all the nations."

Matthew 22:37–39 calls us to love God first, which enables us to love our neighbors.

To walk in God's plan, we are each called to do the things as written in the scriptures listed in Mathew and also walk each day with God in the mission He has architected for each of us.

Do you believe *you* are commissioned for His mission each day? Talk to Him about your three personal questions and ask Him to help you walk with Him for His mission today.

> **Commissioned For His Mission!**
>
> Have you ever thought about how you have been commissioned by God for His mission?
>
> **Commission means:** an instruction, command or duty given to someone.
>
> **Mission means:** an important assignment.
>
> What important assignment have we been instructed to do?
>
> **Matthew 22:37-39** "Love the Lord your God with all your heart and with all your soul and with all your mind. This the first and greatest command. The second is: 'Love your neighbor as yourself.'"

Wait, Receive, and Then Go!

I thank You, Lord, that Your Word is the same yesterday, today, and forever **(Hebrews 13:8)**.

The instructions Jesus Christ gave to His disciples in **Acts 1:4–8** are as applicable for us today as they were when He first spoke them. Read the scripture in context.

We are instructed to *wait* on Him and *receive* the power of the Holy Spirit who equips us to go out *in His name* and *for His name*. These steps in any other order will be fruitless and powerless.

Pray with me: *Oh Lord, help us to understand the importance of waiting for Your instruction, anointing, and direction for our hands and feet! Equip us to share the gospel and be witnesses for You at our homes (an example of our Jerusalem), to our neighbors (an example of our Judea), and in our communities and church bodies (an example of our Samaria). And show us our part in sending Your Word and promise of salvation to the ends of the earth! Help us, God, to wait on You, receive from You, and go as You lead.*

Talk to Him about your three personal questions and how He wants to help you with this instruction for His wonderful glory!

> **Wait, Receive, and Then GO!**
>
> Jesus gave the disciples clear instructions regarding how they would be witnesses to Him. To *wait on* and *receive* the promised baptism of the Holy Spirit and then *GO out* to spread the gospel. This applies to us today.
>
> Acts 1:4,5,8 "...He commanded them not to depart from Jerusalem, but to wait for the Promise of the Father, "which," He said, "You have heard from me; ⁵ for John truly baptized with water, but you shall be baptized with the Holy Spirit not many days from now."
> v.8 "But you shall receive power when the Holy Spirit has come upon you; and you shall be witnesses to Me in Jerusalem, and in all Judea and Samaria, and to the ends of the earth."

His Life *through You!*

Lord, give us a fresh revelation by the spirit of wisdom in the knowledge of You. Amen.

Read **Ephesians 1:17–20**. Have you ever thought about asking God to help you understand "the hope of His calling," the "inheritance in the saints," and the "exceeding greatness of His power toward us who believe"?

There are *no* boundaries in how God wants to allow the *life* of Christ to shine through *your* life according to the hope of His calling and by the power of His Holy Spirit.

Wait on the Lord, *commune* with Him, *walk* with Him, and by the power of the Holy Spirit, the life of Christ who dwells in you will be seen for God's glory through your life.

Talk to your heavenly Father about your three personal questions. Ask for His help to walk in the life of Christ by the power of His Holy Spirit:

His **L**ove

> **I**n you and through you

> **F**or His glory and for

> **E**verlasting life!

Christlike Character

Christ is perfect. He committed no sin **(1 Peter 2:22)**. He was tempted on earth, yet without sin **(Heb. 4:15)**. He became sin by bearing all on the cross so we may become the righteousness of God in Him **(2 Cor. 5:21)**.

In our fleshly weakness and sinful nature, the Holy Spirit does His work to make us more like Him in character. This becomes evident by the fruit of the Spirit manifested in and through our lives **(Matt. 7:20)**.

Let us pray: *Lord, thank You for loving us so much that You suffer long with us to root out sin, refine our character and train us over time in Your ways. Thank You for refining us, molding us, and training us so that the fruit of the Holy Spirit is evident in our lives! Oh Lord, make us more like You so that You can use us for Your glory! Amen.*

Read each of the scriptures referenced in context. Talk to the Lord about your three questions and ask Him to continue to refine you, mold you, and train you for His purpose. Everything and all things always for His glory!

> **Christ-Like Character**
>
> God purifies our hearts, refines us, molds us, and trains us so that fruit of the Holy Spirit is evident in our lives.
>
> 1 Peter 2:22 "who committed no sin, nor was deceit found in His mouth."
>
> Hebrews 4:15 "For we do not have a High Priest who cannot sympathize with our weaknesses, but was in all points tempted as we are, yet without sin."
>
> 2 Corinthians 5:21 "For He made Him who knew no sin to be sin for us that we might become the righteousness of God in Him."
>
> Matthew 7:20 "Therefore, by their fruits you will know them."

Purified Like Silver

Our heavenly Father, mighty King of Kings, and gentle teacher desires to purify our hearts, train us in His truth, and refine and shape us into His vessels so that Christlike fruit is produced through our lives. Thank you, Lord!

He is looking for believers who are willing to surrender to Him in all things and commune with Him; as a result, the Christlike reformation and transformation can take place in their lives.

One way He trains us is through the fiery trials of life, which He can allow for His good purpose. I'm not referring to consequences due to poor decisions made without the Lord, but those trials that God allows to touch us for His good purpose!

Psalm 66:10–12 states, "For you, oh God, have tested us; / You have refined us as silver is refined."

I just love this picture of silver refinement:

The Master Refiner

- builds the fire,
- puts the silver in the pot and allows it to heat,
- scrapes off and removes all the impurities, and
- knows the purification is complete when He sees His reflection in the silver.

Oh, how wonderful that our Master Refiner and Lord God does this through circumstances in our lives for the sake of making us more like Him in character.

I'm so thankful for the promise given in **Psalm 66:10–12:** "But You brought us out to rich *fulfillment*!"

Hallelujah! We are victors in You, Christ Jesus, as You make us more like *You* for Your glorious purpose!

> **Purified Like Silver**
>
> Psalms 66:10-12 "For You, O God, have tested us; You have refined us as silver is refined. You brought us into the net; you laid affliction on our backs. You have caused men to ride over our heads; we went through fire and through water; But You brought us out to rich fulfillment."
>
> "Oh Lord, purify my heart, do Your good work to make the fruit of my life to be more like You."

For His Glory | 155

Trained by the Master Vinedresser

Our faithful Father purifies and refines our hearts, trains us in His truth, and shapes us as His vessels so that we may produce Christlike fruit through our lives for His purpose and glory!

Let's think about how our faithful Father *trains* us.

Read **John 15:1–8.**

I love the picture given to us of Jesus as the true Vine and God our Father as the Vinedresser (or Master Gardener). We are the branches that God our Father prunes in order for us to produce more fruit of the Spirit, and He cuts away branches that do not bear fruit.

The growing and maintenance of grape vines was such a relevant picture in the day and culture in which it was written. We have to think about the vinedressers' job to relate. They plant, sow, and water; they attend to and guide the vines along the training wire, pruning along the way. The path for the vine is carefully planned and placed. The pruning and cutting away of dead branches encourages the increase of the finest fruit, maximizing production. This is a picture of how our heavenly Father trains us in life if we choose to abide in Him. He enables us to produce Christlike fruit through our lives for His purpose and always for His glory!

Talk to our heavenly Father about your three personal questions. Earnestly desire and ask for His training.

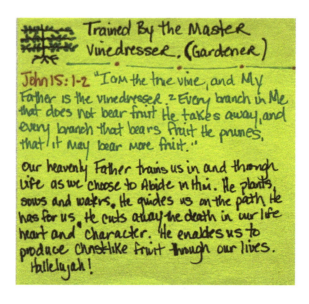

Make Me Your Vessel

Our faithful Father purifies and refines us. He trains us, and He is our Master Potter who molds and shapes us into the beautiful vessels He has envisioned.

God our Father has a purpose He envisions for *you* in His kingdom, and all for His glory! Our molding, shaping, and curing in the fire isn't always easy as a potter may trim away the clay not needed and even flatten the entire lump to start the shaping over again! The refined vessel, freshly shaped, is purified and cured by fire. Yet the work of His hands is not done; the Master Potter continues to make the vessel beautiful and unique for His purpose **(Isa. 64:8)**.

Read the context of the scripture in **Isaiah 64** and **Jeremiah 18:1–11**.

Let us pray for His good work in us: *Make me Your vessel, Lord! Do all that is needed to make me useful and beautiful for Your purpose. Fan a flame in my heart, Lord, to earnestly desire Your shaping and molding so that I may be used and poured out for all You want to do through my life, Lord. All things and always for Your glory, Lord. Amen.*

Talk with our heavenly Father about your three personal questions.

> **Make Me Your Vessel**
>
> Isaiah 64:8 "But now, O Lord, You are our Father; We are the clay, and You our potter; And all we are the work of Your hand."
>
> Read Jeremiah 18:1-11 for context.
>
> Jeremiah 18:4-6 "And the vessel that he made of clay was marred in the hand of the potter; so he made it again into another vessel, as it seemed good to the potter to make. Then, the word of the Lord came to me, saying 'O house of Isreal, can I not do with you as this potter? says the Lord. "Look, as the clay is in the potter's hand, so are you in My hand, O house of Isreal!"
>
> "Lord, shape me and mold me for Your Purpose!"

Produce Christlike Fruit through Me

We thank our heavenly Father who does His good work in and through us for His glory. Thank Him as He makes you more Christlike in character over time and in all God-orchestrated circumstances.

He purifies and refines our hearts. He trains us patiently over time and in all God-orchestrated circumstance. He shapes us into His precious, beloved, and purposeful vessels. As a result, He changes our character to be Christlike in Him. We will never be perfectly sinless like Christ was on earth (and still is today). This is why we need our Savior so.

Read through each scripture in context within **Galatians, Matthew,** and **Philippians** (provided below).

We have a wonderful Savior who wipes our sin away and sets about doing His good work in us. Each of our journeys may look a little different, but we can rest assured that we will always recognize God's beloved because of the evidenced fruit of His Holy Spirit in each of our lives **(Matt. 7:16)**.

Our faithful Father will complete and perform His good work in us until our appointed last day on this earth **(Phil. 1:6)**.

To God be the glory, and everything for His glory! Amen.

Talk with Him about your three personal questions and thank Him.

By God's grace, a second volume of devotionals will be published. Be on the watch for the next publication!

CPSIA information can be obtained
at www.ICGtesting.com
Printed in the USA
BVHW092138301022
650606BV00005B/17